Southern Living

kids cookbook

Southern Living
kids cookbook

COMPILED AND EDITED BY
ELIZABETH TALIAFERRO

OXMOOR
HOUSE®

©2007 by Oxmoor House, Inc.
Book Division of Southern Progress Corporation
P. O. Box 2262, Birmingham, Alabama 35201-2262

Southern Living® is a federally registered trademark belonging
to Southern Living, Inc.

ISBN-13: 978-0-8487-3178-6
ISBN-10: 0-8487-3178-6
Library of Congress Control Number: 2006908795
Printed in People's Republic of China
Second Printing 2008

Editor in Chief: Nancy Fitzpatrick Wyatt
Executive Editor: Susan Carlisle Payne
Managing Editor: Allison Long Lowery

SOUTHERN LIVING KIDS' COOKBOOK

Editor: Elizabeth Taliaferro
Assistant Editor: Julie Christopher
Copy Editor: Jacqueline Giovanelli
Editorial Assistant: Rachel Quinlivan, R.D.
Senior Designer: Emily Albright Parrish
Photography Director: Jim Bathie
Senior Photo Stylist: Kay E. Clarke
Associate Photo Stylist: Katherine G. Eckert
Director, Test Kitchens: Elizabeth Tyler Austin
Food Stylist: Kelley Self Wilton
Test Kitchens Staff: Kathleen Royal Phillips,
Catherine Crowell Steele,
Ashley T. Strickland
Director of Production: Laura Lockhart
Senior Production Manager: Greg A. Amason
Production Assistant: Faye Porter Bonner

CONTRIBUTORS

Indexer: Mary Ann Laurens
Interns: Jill Baughman, Amy Edgerton,
Amelia Heying
Editorial Assistant: Laura K. Womble
Photographers: Beau Gustafson, Lee Harrelson
Photo Stylist: Leigh Anne Montgomery

To order additional publications, call 1-800-765-6400.
For more books to enrich your life, visit **oxmoorhouse.com**
To search, savor, and share thousands of recipes, visit **myrecipes.com**

Cover: Tuna Fish In-A-Fish (page 88), Elephant Ears (page 44),
Got Milk Shakes! (page 30), Beary Good Rolls (page 173),
Viva les Galettes (page 160)
page 1: Carrot-Orange Caricature (page 169)
page 2: Sunny Carrot, Pizza, and Plain Jane Muffins (page 34)

How we analyze recipes

• If a recipe has a range of amounts, we analyze with the first amount.

• If a recipe gives more than 1 choice for an ingredient, we analyze with the first choice.

• Decorations, accompaniments, and optional ingredients aren't included in the nutritional analysis.

• When a recipe says to cook pasta according to package directions, we analyze adding 1 tablespoon of salt to the water for every 16 ounces of dry pasta.

• We added a banner labeled *good for you* by recipes that are low in refined sugar, calories, fat, saturated fat, and sodium. These recipes contain foods kids need but often don't get enough of like fruits, vegetables, and/or dairy products.

CONTENTS

WELCOME

Dear Grown-Ups,

Kids love to cook! It enhances their self-esteem, gives them a sense of accomplishment, and teaches them all sorts of practical knowledge. And the best part—it's just plain fun!

The *Southern Living* Kids' Cookbook is all about kids and grown-ups cooking together. Before you head to the kitchen, enjoy exploring the book with the children in your life. Read it together during a story time or at bedtime to pique their curiosity.

The recipes are intended for children ages 4 through 12. Of course, no one knows your kids like you, so you'll be able to determine what recipes are appropriate for them to prepare. And remember, all kids need supervision while cooking, so never leave them unattended.

Go ahead! Pick a recipe, shop for it, and start cooking with the kids. You'll be surprised at how much joy everyone will have creating and serving home-cooked food.

Hey Kids,

This cookbook shows you how to make all kinds of yummy food. Plus it's cool to read, just like books with pictures and stories. Start off by reading *All About Cooking* to find out lots of important things that will keep you safe in the kitchen and help you become a great cook.

After you read that chapter, flip through the rest of the book. Read the recipes that look good to you. Decide on several you'd like to make, and share them with a grown-up. The two of you can decide which recipes to choose. Have fun!

Finding recipes that are just right is so simple—look for these colorful banners. They quickly tell you something special about making or serving the recipe.

MAKE-AHEAD	a recipe that can be made hours or even days before serving
SUPERFAST & EASY	a simple recipe taking no more than 15 minutes to put together
BREAKFAST BOOSTER	a high-protein, low-sugar recipe perfect for first thing in the morning
NO COOK	a recipe requiring no cooking—not even in the microwave
ON-THE-GO SNACK	a recipe that travels well and is easy to eat with your fingers
GOOD FOR YOU	a recipe that's low in refined sugar, fat, saturated fat, calories, and sodium
UP TO THE CHALLENGE?	a challenging recipe for older children
JUST FOR FUN	a recipe that's silly to make and eat
LUNCHBOX FAVORITE	a recipe that packs well in an insulated lunchbox
EXTRA-EASY	a recipe that's simple and needs little attention as it cooks

aLL aBOUT COOKING

Cooking Tools and Equipment Before you begin cooking, explore your kitchen to find these common items. That way you can easily locate the equipment you need when you're ready to start cooking.

measuring cups
(for dry ingredients)

measuring cup (for liquids)

measuring spoons

veggie peeler, wooden
spoon, wire whisk

electric mixer

kitchen shears

grater

mixing bowls

pastry blender and brushes

colander

rubber spatula, tongs

saucepan with lid

nonstick skillet   Dutch oven with lid   baking sheets   baking pans

How to Follow a Recipe
To get food to turn out just right, it's best to prepare a recipe in the order listed below.

1 **Read the recipe** from the beginning to the end.

2 **Check the cook and prep times**, and make sure you'll be home long enough to make the recipe. Time labeled as "other" accounts for things like chilling, freezing, rising, cooling, and standing. You can do other things during this time.

3 **Gather all the ingredients** you'll need from the ingredient list. Ingredients in this book are in bold type so you can easily identify them.

4 **Gather all the equipment and tools** you'll need to prepare the recipe. Reading through the recipe's directions is helpful for this. Sometimes they tell you exactly what you'll need but sometimes you can decide.

5 **Prepare the ingredients** as the ingredient list in the recipe describes. This may include chopping, slicing, or measuring. This is also a good time to open packages or boxes of food.

Understanding Cook Time

Keep Up with Time
You can always watch the clock, but most cooks like using a kitchen timer in case they get distracted. Watching the time is important because it will prevent over- or under-cooking. Lots of ovens and microwaves have digital timers built right in.

Check for Doneness
Deciding when your recipe is ready depends on your good judgment and a well-written recipe. Our recipes give you a time and a sign you can see. Use them both to help you decide when the recipe has cooked properly.

Caution! Caution! Caution!
Just as some foods become done, they're very, very hot. It's always a good idea to let them cool at least a minute or two before tasting so you won't burn your mouth.

Kitchen Safety
To prevent accidents and avoid getting hurt in the kitchen, be smart and follow the tips listed below.

- Clear off and clean a space on the countertop big enough to work easily.
- Roll up your shirtsleeves and tie loose hair back to keep them out of the way.
- Wash your hands with soap and warm water before and after you touch food, especially raw meat, chicken, fish, and eggs.
- Clean up spills, tools, and work surfaces as you go.
- Always have an adult close by in case you need help or have questions.
- Be careful with sharp knives and all cooking tools.
- Angle pot handles toward the back of the stovetop so you won't knock off a pot accidentally.
- Stay in the kitchen when the stovetop or oven is on.
- If you're using a gas stovetop, never reach over an open flame. All stovetops can stay hot after turning them off, especially electric ones. So don't touch them or put anything on them that might burn, like paper towels or oven mitts.
- Always use oven mitts when moving hot dishes in and out of the oven or microwave.

Washing fruits and vegetables

Place produce in a colander, and rinse thoroughly under cool running water. Scrub tough-skinned vegetables like potatoes and carrots with a vegetable brush, and pat them dry with paper towels. Skip the scrubbing on fragile produce like tomatoes, strawberries, grapes and green peas. Instead, turn them out onto paper towels after a thorough rinsing, and let them air dry.

Beating bacteria

Here are three important rules for keeping food safe to eat. If you don't follow them, bacteria that might make you sick could grow in the food.

1. Once food has been cooked, keep it hot until you're ready to serve it. If you're not planning to eat it immediately, refrigerate it right away to prevent germs from growing. And when you do reheat it, make certain it gets hot and steamy again.

2. Keep foods that are supposed to be cold in the refrigerator or freezer until you're ready to use them. The safest way to thaw frozen food is to put it in the refrigerator for several hours or overnight.

3. Prepared food should never be eaten if it sits out at room temperature longer than 2 hours. And if food is outdoors and it's warm, like at a picnic or backyard cookout, don't eat it if it's been sitting out longer than 1 hour.

A Perfectly Proper Place Setting

For each person, put a plate on the table or placemat in front of a chair. Put the fork on the left side of the plate with a napkin. Put the knife on the right side of the plate with the blade facing toward the plate. Put a spoon to the right of the knife. The glass goes just above the tip of the knife. ◆

Kid-Tested and Approved

We appreciate these children and their moms! We asked for their help to test all kinds of new recipes from this book. They enthusiastically prepared the foods and took great pride in adding helpful comments, tips, and ideas. Thanks kids for a job well done!

first row: Ward, Taylor, Trent; **second row:** Luke and Andrew; **third row:** Sarah, Will, Charlestan, Sarah **fourth row:** James and Seth; **fifth row:** Taylor and Hannah

How to Cut Up Ingredients
To cut up ingredients, you'll need a sharp knife and a cutting board. Here are some directions for foods you'll use often.

To Chop Onion
1. Cut an onion in half through the root end, and peel away the dry outer layer. Place the onion halves flat on the cutting board, and trim away the stem end.
2. Cut each half lengthwise into slices, cutting to but not through the root end. That way the onion won't fall apart into slices.
3. Cut across the slices crosswise to finish the chopping. Be careful to keep your fingers out of the way.

To Mince Garlic
1. Separate a head of garlic into cloves.
2. Press a garlic clove by mashing it under the weight of your hand on a chef's knife. Then slip the peel off the garlic clove with your fingers.
3. Cut the clove lengthwise into thin slices. Cut across the slices crosswise to finish mincing.

To Slice, Cube, or Dice a Potato
1. Peel the potato, if you'd like. Hold the potato steady on a cutting board. Beginning at one end, cut the potato into slices.
2. To cube the potato, stack several slices. Cut the stack into ½-inch slices lengthwise, holding it carefully to keep the stack in place.
3. To finish cubing, turn the stack, and cut it into ½-inch slices crosswise.
4. To dice the potato, cut the slices and stacks very thin.

To Peel a Carrot and Cut into Julienne Strips
1. Hold the carrot firmly at the stem. Using a vegetable peeler, peel away the skin by scraping the peeler along the length of the carrot. Always scrape by pushing the peeler away from you.
2. Cut away the skinny tip and stem end of each carrot. Cut each carrot in half crosswise.
3. Cut the carrot pieces into slices. Stack the slices, and cut lengthwise into thin strips.

julienne

cube

chop

dice

mince

How to Tell the Difference Between Cuts

It's helpful to know that small pieces of food take less time to cook than larger pieces of food.

Julienne: To cut food into thin, uniform matchsticks that are 2 to 3 inches long and ⅛ to ¼ inch wide.

Cube: To cut food into square pieces ½ to 1 inch or larger.

Dice: To cut food into square pieces ranging from ¼ to ½ inch.

Chop: To cut food roughly into small, irregular pieces.

Mince: To cut food into very fine, irregular pieces.

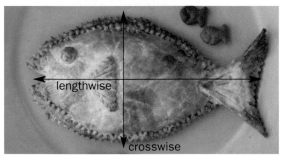

lengthwise

crosswise

To Cut Crosswise and Lengthwise

These words can be confusing, even to grown-ups. Just remember:

- If a recipe tells you to cut something lengthwise, that means along the length.
- If it says to cut it crosswise, that mean across the width.

Knife Know-How

- Sharp knives are better than dull knives because they cut easily and with more control.
- A knife should fit your hand. Just like running with shoes that are too big can be risky, so is using a knife big enough for a grown-up. A knife fits properly when you can comfortably hold it in your hand without feeling like you might cut yourself.
- Wood or plastic cutting boards are best to cut on. Other surfaces can be slippery. To avoid spreading germs, it's best to have two cutting boards, a wood or plastic one for fruits and vegetables and another plastic one for raw meat, poultry, and fish. ⓐ
- Place the item you are cutting on the cutting board, and hold it securely, being careful to keep your fingers out of the knife's way. And as you cut, always move the knife away from your body. Ⓑ
- It's very important to wash cutting boards and knives after you use them because some foods, like raw meat, chicken, fish, and eggs, may contain bacteria that can make you sick. Carefully wash the cutting boards with hot, soapy water after each use. Rinse with clear water, and pat them dry with clean paper towels. It's OK to wash nonporous cutting boards, like acrylic or plastic, in the dishwasher.

How to Prepare Ingredients
Our recipes tell you exactly how to prepare ingredients. Some things are done so frequently, we thought it was important to talk about them here.

To Crack Eggs
Tap the middle of the egg firmly against the rim of a bowl. Holding the cracked egg over the bowl, pull the two halves of the shell apart, and let the egg fall into the bowl. Use large eggs for the recipes in this book.

To Shred a Block of Cheese ⬆
Starting at the top of the grater, use firm, downward strokes to rub the block of cheese over the large holes of the grater. As the block of cheese becomes smaller, adjust your hand to keep your fingers away from the holes because the cutting edges are sharp!

To Separate the Egg White and Yolk
If you need only an egg white or an egg yolk, crack the egg, as directed above. Then, using your clean fingers, scoop up the egg yolk, letting the white part drain back into the bowl.

To Lightly Beat Eggs
Whisk the eggs in a bowl with a wire whisk or a fork using a quick circular motion until they're smooth and light yellow throughout.

To Soften Butter and Cream Cheese
Unwrap the butter or cream cheese. Let it stand at room temperature until it's soft enough to smush when you press it gently with your finger.

To Grate Citrus Rind ⬆
Using short, downward strokes, rub the fruit over a grater with small holes. Turn the fruit as you go so you'll only grate the outermost part. Avoid the white part (pith) underneath because it tastes bitter. Be careful to keep your fingers away from the holes as you grate!

How to Measure Ingredients

It's important to measure ingredients properly so you can be sure you're using the correct amount. There are two types of measuring cups—one for dry ingredients and one for wet ingredients. Dry measuring cups are usually metal or plastic and come in a set with several different sizes. Liquid measuring cups are usually glass and have a pouring spout. (See page 7 for photos.)

To measure ¼ cup or more of a dry ingredient ▶
- Spoon the ingredient into the right size dry measuring cup until it's more than full. Don't pack down the ingredient unless it's brown sugar, which should be firmly packed. Using the flat side of a table knife, level off the ingredient until it's even with the rim of the measuring cup.

To measure a small amount or less than ¼ cup of a dry ingredient
- Dip the right size measuring spoon into the ingredient, and fill it until it's more than full. Using the back of a table knife, level it off until it's even with the rim of the measuring spoon.

To measure ¼ cup or more of a wet ingredient ▶
- Place a liquid measuring cup on the countertop. Bend down so that the measuring lines are at your eye level. Carefully pour the liquid into the measuring cup until the liquid reaches the correct line of measure.

To measure a small amount or less than ¼ cup of a wet ingredient
- Carefully pour the ingredient into a measuring spoon until it reaches the rim. If the wet ingredient is sticky, like honey, spray the inside of the measuring spoon with vegetable cooking spray before measuring so the ingredient will slide out easily.

To measure ingredients that aren't exactly liquid or dry
- Measure ingredients like barbecue sauce, ketchup, mayonnaise, honey, sour cream, and molasses in dry measuring cups. Use dry measuring cups for shortening, cream cheese, and peanut butter, too. These firmer kinds of ingredients need to be pressed into the cup with a small spatula to force out all the air pockets, and then leveled with a knife.

To measure butter
- Butter is marked on the wrapper with measuring lines. Place the stick on a cutting board, and line up a small, sharp knife at the correct measuring line. Cut straight down through the wrapped butter to cut off the right amount.

math you'll use

Dry ingredients
3 teaspoons = 1 tablespoon
4 tablespoons = ¼ cup
5 tablespoons plus 1 teaspoon = ⅓ cup
8 tablespoons = ½ cup
16 tablespoons = 1 cup

Liquid ingredients
1 cup = 8 fluid ounces
2 cups = 1 pint
2 pints = 1 quart
4 quarts = 1 gallon

Ingredients in weight
4 ounces = ¼ pound
8 ounces = ½ pound
12 ounces = ¾ pound
16 ounces = 1 pound

Fairy Princess
Wands, page 24

SNACKS & BEVERAGES

GOOD FOR YOU

LUNCHBOX FAVORITE

ROOTIN' TOOTIN' FRUIT SALSA

Need to rustle up a healthy snack? There's nothing like a low-fat fruit salsa to give you energy and vitamins to boot!

1 pint **fresh strawberries,** stems removed, and berries chopped

1 **large banana,** peeled and chopped

1 **medium-size Red Delicious apple,** unpeeled and chopped

2 **kiwifruit,** peeled and chopped

2 tablespoons fresh **lemon** juice

¼ cup **sugar**

½ teaspoon **ground cinnamon**

¼ teaspoon **ground nutmeg**

Cinnamon Crisps

1 • *Stir** together first 4 ingredients in a big bowl. *Drizzle** lemon juice over fruit; stir gently to coat. Sprinkle sugar, cinnamon, and nutmeg over fruit; stir gently.

• Cover with plastic wrap, and *chill** fruit salsa in the refrigerator at least 30 minutes.

• Serve fruit salsa with Cinnamon Crisps. Makes 2⅔ cups fruit salsa

FOR ⅓ CUP FRUIT SALSA AND 4 CINNAMON CRISPS: CALORIES 136 (12% from fat); FAT 1.8g (sat 0.5g, mono 0g, poly 0.1g); PROTEIN 3.2g; CARB 29.1g; FIBER 3.2g; CHOL 0mg; IRON 0.4mg; SODIUM 18mg; CALC 17mg

CINNAMON CRISPS

4 (8-inch) **flour tortillas**

Vegetable cooking spray

2 tablespoons **sugar**

¾ teaspoon **ground cinnamon**

1 • *Preheat** oven to 350°.

2 • Spray one side of each tortilla with vegetable cooking spray. Stir together sugar and cinnamon in a small bowl. Sprinkle sugar mixture over each tortilla. Cut tortillas into boot shapes with a 4-inch cookie cutter or into 8 wedges. Place about 1 inch apart on an ungreased baking sheet.

• *Bake** at 350° for 6 to 8 minutes or until lightly browned. Remove baking sheet from the oven using oven mitts. Cool. Makes 32 cinnamon crisps

FOR 4 CINNAMON CRISPS: CALORIES 66 (20% from fat); FAT 1.5g (sat 0.5g, mono 0g, poly 0g); PROTEIN 2.5g; CARB 11.3g; FIBER 1.1g; CHOL 0mg; IRON 0.1mg; SODIUM 17mg; CALC 3mg

* see glossary

PEANUTTY DIP

This snack comes together so quickly you can make it right after you come home from school. Measure each ingredient in a dry measuring cup.

1 cup **vanilla low-fat yogurt**

½ cup **powdered sugar**

¼ cup **creamy peanut butter**

1 • *Whisk** all ingredients in a medium bowl until smooth. Serve with fresh fruit, graham cracker sticks, or pretzel twists. Makes 1⅓ cups dip

FOR 1 TABLESPOON: CALORIES 39 (39% from fat); FAT 1.7g (sat 0.4g, mono 0g, poly 0g); PROTEIN 1.2g; CARB 5.1g; FIBER 0.2g; CHOL 1mg; IRON 0.1mg; SODIUM 21mg; CALC 16mg

* see glossary

**Prep: 5 min.
Other: 2 hrs.**

DUNKIN' DILL DIP

Cherry tomatoes make fun, healthy lollipops to eat with this dip. Pierce each tomato with a small, pointed knife, and then push in the popsicle stick.

1 (8-ounce) **container light sour cream**

¾ cup **reduced-fat mayonnaise**

2 teaspoons **dried parsley**

2 teaspoons **dried dillweed**

2 teaspoons **dried minced onion**

¼ teaspoon **seasoned salt**

1 • *Stir** together all ingredients in a medium bowl. Cover with plastic wrap, and *chill** in the refrigerator at least 2 hours. Serve with fresh vegetables. Makes 1½ cups dip

FOR 1 TABLESPOON: CALORIES 38 (85% from fat); FAT 3.6g (sat 1.2g, mono 0.3g, poly 0g); PROTEIN 0.3g; CARB 1g; FIBER 0g; CHOL 6mg; IRON 0.1mg; SODIUM 79mg; CALC 12mg

* see glossary

CHOCOLATY CARAMEL PRETZELS

Pouring the melted caramel into a 2-cup glass measuring cup gives you a nice, deep pool to dip the long pretzels into.

1 (14-ounce) **package caramels**

2 tablespoons **water**

2 cups **chopped pecans or unsalted peanuts**

1 (10-ounce) **package pretzel rods**

1½ cups **semisweet chocolate morsels**

3 (2-ounce) **chocolate bark coating squares**

1 • Unwrap caramels, and put in a medium microwave-safe bowl. Pour 2 tablespoons water over caramels. Microwave at MEDIUM-HIGH (70% power) 2 minutes or until caramels look like they're just beginning to melt. *Stir** caramel mixture until smooth, and pour into a 2-cup glass measuring cup.

2 • Place pecans on a shallow plate. Dip a pretzel rod into the melted caramel. When you lift it out, let the excess caramel drip back into the cup. Roll the caramel-coated pretzel in pecans while the caramel is still soft. Place it on a wax paper-lined baking sheet.
• Do the same thing all over again with the rest of the pretzels, caramel, and pecans. If the caramel begins to thicken while you're dipping, microwave it at HIGH 20 to 30 seconds or until thin enough for dipping again. When you finish dipping all the pretzels, *chill** them in the refrigerator about 10 minutes or until the caramel is no longer soft.

3 • Place chocolate morsels and chocolate squares in a medium microwave-safe bowl. Microwave at HIGH 1 minute or until chocolate looks like it's just beginning to melt. Stir chocolate until smooth.
• *Drizzle** melted chocolate from a spoon over each pecan-coated pretzel, or dip the pretzel into chocolate, if you'd like. Return pretzels to the wax paper-lined baking sheets, and chill in the refrigerator about 10 minutes or until chocolate hardens.
• Store in an airtight container up to 1 week. Makes about 27 pretzels

FOR 1 PRETZEL: CALORIES 228 (52% from fat); FAT 13.2g (sat 4g, mono 5.7g, poly 2.7g); PROTEIN 3.4g; CARB 28.6g; FIBER 1.9g; CHOL 1mg; IRON 1.2mg; SODIUM 159mg; CALC 35mg

* see glossary

GRANOLA TRIANGLES

MAKE-AHEAD
ON-THE-GO SNACK
LUNCHBOX FAVORITE

You'll love these extrachewy granola snacks with just a few chocolate morsels tossed in. Use chunky peanut butter for added crunch.

2½ cups **crisp rice cereal** (we used Rice Krispies)

2 cups uncooked **quick-cooking oats**

½ cup **raisins**

½ cup firmly packed **brown sugar**

½ cup **light corn syrup**

½ cup **creamy peanut butter**

1 teaspoon **vanilla extract**

½ cup **milk chocolate morsels**

Vegetable cooking spray

1 • Combine first 3 ingredients in a big bowl; set aside.

2 • *Stir** together brown sugar and syrup in a small saucepan. Bring mixture to a *boil** over medium-high heat, stirring constantly. Remove from heat, and stir in peanut butter and vanilla until smooth.
• Pour peanut butter mixture over cereal mixture, stirring until coated. Let stand 10 minutes to cool.

3 • Stir chocolate morsels into cereal mixture. Spoon mixture into a lightly *greased** 13- x 9-inch pan. Spray your hands with cooking spray, and press the mixture into an even layer. Cut into 12 squares. Cut each square in half to form a triangle.
• Store in an airtight container up to 1 week. Makes 2 dozen triangles

FOR 1 TRIANGLE: CALORIES 140 (30% from fat); FAT 4.7g (sat 1.4g, mono 0.1g, poly 0.2g); PROTEIN 2.9g; CARB 23.2g; FIBER 1.1g; CHOL 2mg; IRON 3.7mg; SODIUM 61mg; CALC 10mg

* see glossary

RANCH SNACK MUNCHIES*

SUPERFAST & EASY
NO COOK
ON-THE-GO SNACK

Use the biggest mixing bowl you can find to make this recipe.

6 cups **corn-and-rice cereal** (we used Crispix)

1 (10-ounce) **package oyster crackers**

4 cups **small pretzel twists**

¼ cup **vegetable oil**

2 tablespoons **dried dillweed**

1 (1-ounce) **envelope Ranch dressing mix**

1
- Combine first 3 ingredients in a big bowl; set aside.
- *Whisk** vegetable oil, dillweed, and dressing mix in a small bowl until smooth. *Drizzle** over cereal mixture; *stir** gently to coat.
- Store mixture in an airtight container up to 1 week. Makes 4 quarts snack mix

FOR ½ CUP: CALORIES 95 (27% from fat); FAT 2.9g (sat 0.2g, mono 0.8g, poly 0.8g); PROTEIN 1.4g; CARB 16.1g; FIBER 0.2g; CHOL 0mg; IRON 2.7mg; SODIUM 314mg; CALC 4mg

* see glossary

Prep: 22 min.
Cook: 2 min., 30 sec.
Other: 1 hr., 15 min.

FAIRY PRINCESS WANDS

There's magic in the air when you serve these delicious treats. Make a wish and watch them disappear!

8 cups **corn puff cereal** (we used Kellogg's Corn Pops)

1 (12-ounce) **package white chocolate morsels**

½ cup **light corn syrup**

¼ cup **butter or margarine**

Vegetable cooking spray

12 (12-inch) **lollipop sticks**

⅓ cup **white chocolate morsels**

Sugar sprinkles (optional)

1
- Pour cereal into a big bowl, and set aside.
- Combine white chocolate morsels, corn syrup, and butter in a medium-size microwave-safe bowl. Microwave at HIGH 2 minutes; *stir** until smooth.
- *Drizzle** white chocolate mixture over cereal, stirring to coat. Spoon mixture into a lightly *greased** 15- x 10-inch jelly-roll pan. Spray your hands with cooking spray, and press the mixture into an even layer. Let stand 15 minutes.

2
- Cut cereal mixture into stars with a 4-inch cookie cutter. Place stars on a wax paper-lined baking sheet. Cover and *chill** in the refrigerator 1 hour or until firm. (Store excess cereal mixture in an airtight container for snacking.)

3 Assemble the wands:
- Have a grown-up insert a lollipop stick into each star.
- Place ⅓ cup white chocolate morsels in a zip-top freezer bag. Partially seal bag, and set upright in a small microwave-safe measuring cup. Microwave at HIGH 20 to 30 seconds or just until chips melt. *Snip** a tiny hole in 1 corner of bag to create a small opening. Drizzle melted chocolate over stars, and sprinkle with sugar sprinkles, if you'd like. Let stand until firm.
- Store wands in an airtight container up to 1 week. Makes 12 wands

FOR 1 WAND: CALORIES 171 (46% from fat); FAT 8.8g (sat 6.9g, mono 0.5g, poly 0.1g); PROTEIN 0.7g; CARB 24.2g; FIBER 0.7g; CHOL 5mg; IRON 0.1mg; SODIUM 44mg; CALC 2mg

* see glossary

Tip: You'll find lollipop sticks at an arts and crafts store.

SPICY PITA CHIPS

These pita chips are crisp like potato chips but much healthier because they're baked, not fried.

4 (6-inch) **pita bread rounds**

Butter-flavored cooking spray

1 teaspoon **garlic powder**

½ teaspoon **sugar**

½ teaspoon **paprika**

¼ teaspoon **ground red pepper**

1 • *Preheat** oven to 300°.

2 • Cut each pita into 2 circles using kitchen shears. Cut each circle into 6 wedges. Arrange wedges, smooth sides down, in a single layer on a big baking sheet. Spray wedges with cooking spray.
   • *Stir** together garlic powder and remaining ingredients; sprinkle on pita wedges.

3 • *Bake** at 300° for 15 minutes or until chips are lightly browned and crisp.
   • Remove baking sheet from the oven using oven mitts. Cool.
   • Store pita chips in an airtight container up to 1 week. Makes 4 dozen pita chips

FOR 4 CHIPS: CALORIES 110 (0% from fat); FAT 0g (sat 0g, mono 0g, poly 0g); PROTEIN 4.8g; CARB 22.8g; FIBER 0.8g; CHOL 0mg; IRON 1.9mg; SODIUM 107mg; CALC 27mg

* see glossary

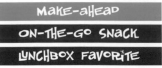

Prep: 5 min.

TUTTi FRUiTY SMOOTHiES

There's no need to thaw the berries or peaches for this recipe. In fact, the frozen fruit helps make the smoothie thick and creamy.

1 (8-ounce) **carton vanilla low-fat yogurt**

1 **ripe banana,** peeled and cut into chunks

½ cup **orange juice**

1 teaspoon **vanilla extract**

4 **frozen unsweetened whole strawberries,** ½ cup **frozen blueberries,** or ½ cup **frozen sliced peaches**

1 • Place first 4 ingredients in a blender; top with cover, and pulse until smooth. Remove cover, and add strawberries, blueberries, or peaches. Top with cover, and process until smooth, stopping to scrape down sides, if you need to. Serve immediately. Makes 2 servings

FOR 1 SERVING: CALORIES 194 (10% from fat); FAT 2.1g (sat 1.1g, mono 0.1g, poly 0.1g); PROTEIN 5.9g; CARB 38.6g; FIBER 2.1g; CHOL 7mg; IRON 0.4mg; SODIUM 69mg; CALC 180mg

LEMONADE BY THE GLASS

This recipe is the real thing and bears little resemblance to the stuff made from a powdered mix. Your hands will smell citrusy fresh when you're done, too.

2 **lemons**

3 tablespoons **sugar**

¾ cup **water**

1 • Gently roll each lemon on countertop to soften. **a** Cut lemons in half, and remove lemon juice using a *juicer**. **B** Combine sugar, 3 tablespoons fresh lemon juice, and 3 tablespoons water in a tall glass; **C** *stir** gently with a small spoon until sugar *dissolves**. **D** Add remaining water, **E** and stir well. Fill glass with ice. Serve immediately. Makes 1 serving

FOR **1 SERVING**: CALORIES 157 (0% from fat); FAT 0g (sat 0g, mono 0g, poly 0g); PROTEIN 0.2g; CARB 41.4g; FIBER 0.2g; CHOL 0mg; IRON 0mg; SODIUM 0mg; CALC 4mg

* see glossary

GOT MILK SHAKES!

Plan a movie and milk shake night and invite your friends over for a do-it-yourself milk shake making party. Guests can pick their favorite flavors and decorate their glasses using the instructions below (see Spiffed-Up Milk Shakes).

2⅓ cups packed **vanilla ice cream**

⅔ cup **milk**

½ teaspoon **vanilla extract**

1 • Place all ingredients in a blender; top with cover, and process until smooth. Serve immediately. Makes 3 servings

FOR 1 SERVING: CALORIES 241 (49% from fat); FAT 13g (sat 8g, mono 3.7g, poly 0.5g); PROTEIN 5.3g; CARB 26.7g; FIBER 0g; CHOL 51mg; IRON 0.1mg; SODIUM 104mg; CALC 193mg

Strawberry Milk Shakes:

• Add ½ cup strawberry jam along with other ingredients to blender, and continue as directed.

FOR 1 SERVING: CALORIES 374 (31% from fat); FAT 13g (sat 8g, mono 3.7g, poly 0.5g); PROTEIN 5.3g; CARB 61.4g; FIBER 0g; CHOL 51mg; IRON 0.1mg; SODIUM 104mg; CALC 193mg

Chocolate Milk Shakes:

• Add ½ cup chocolate syrup along with other ingredients to blender, and continue as directed.

FOR 1 SERVING: CALORIES 374 (31% from fat); FAT 13g (sat 8g, mono 3.7g, poly 0.5g); PROTEIN 6.7g; CARB 58.7g; FIBER 0g; CHOL 51mg; IRON 0.6mg; SODIUM 137mg; CALC 193mg

Spiffed-Up Milk Shakes: Microwave 1 cup semisweet chocolate morsels in a shallow dish at HIGH 1 minute or until they look like they're just beginning to melt. Stir the chocolate until it's smooth. Dip the rim of each glass into the melted chocolate and sprinkle with colored sugar or sprinkles. Without touching the chocolate, let the glass stand for about 5 minutes. Once the chocolate hardens, you're ready to make the milk shakes.

Cinnamon Raisin
Bread, page 42

BREADS

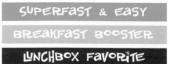

PLAIN JANE MUFFINS

A warm muffin and a spot of tea will entice your imagination to take you to a faraway place without leaving the comforts of home. Pick your favorite muffin from three tasty varieties.

2 cups **self-rising flour**
⅓ cup **sugar**
1 cup **milk**
¼ cup **vegetable oil**
1 **large egg**

1 • *Preheat** oven to 400°.

2 Prepare the batter:
- *Stir** together flour and sugar in a medium bowl; make a *well** in center of mixture using a wooden spoon.
- *Whisk** milk, oil, and egg in a small bowl until smooth. Pour milk mixture into well, and stir just until moistened.
- Spoon *batter** into lightly *greased** muffin pans, filling three-fourths full.

3 • *Bake** at 400° for 18 minutes or until golden.
- Remove muffin pans from the oven using oven mitts. *Invert** muffins onto a wire rack. Serve warm. Makes 1 dozen muffins

FOR 1 MUFFIN: CALORIES 154 (34% from fat); FAT 5.9g (sat 1g, mono 2.3g, poly 2.2g); PROTEIN 3.2g; CARB 22g; FIBER 0.6g; CHOL 20mg; IRON 1.1mg; SODIUM 279mg; CALC 96mg

Sunny Carrot Muffins:
- Stir ½ cup raisins, ½ cup shredded carrot, ¾ teaspoon ground cinnamon, and ¼ teaspoon ground nutmeg into flour mixture in step 2 before making a well. Continue as directed.

FOR 1 MUFFIN: CALORIES 174 (31% from fat); FAT 6g (sat 1g, mono 2.4g, poly 2.2g); PROTEIN 3.5g; CARB 27.3g; FIBER 1g; CHOL 20mg; IRON 1.2mg; SODIUM 282mg; CALC 102mg

Pizza Muffins:
- Count out 40 pepperoni slices, and make several stacks. Cut pepperoni stacks into quarters. Stir pepperoni, 1 cup shredded sharp Cheddar cheese, and ¼ teaspoon garlic powder into flour mixture in step 2 before making a well. Continue with step 2. After filling muffin cups with batter, sprinkle each with 1 teaspoon grated Parmesan cheese. Continue as directed.

FOR 1 MUFFIN: CALORIES 227 (48% from fat); FAT 12g (sat 4.4g, mono 3.7g, poly 2.4g); PROTEIN 7.2g; CARB 22.7g; FIBER 0.7g; CHOL 37mg; IRON 1.2mg; SODIUM 478mg; CALC 182mg

* see glossary

SUPERFAST & EASY
BREAKFAST BOOSTER
LUNCHBOX FAVORITE

Plain Jane
Muffin

Pizza
Muffin

Sunny Carrot
Muffin

PERFECT PANCAKES

The cool thing about this pancake batter is that you can make waffles out of it, too.

2 cups **buttermilk**

⅓ cup **vegetable oil**

2 **large eggs**

2¼ cups **self-rising flour**

2 tablespoons **sugar**

½ teaspoon **baking soda**

1 • Place buttermilk, oil, and eggs in a blender; add flour, sugar, and baking soda. Top with cover, and process just until smooth, stopping to scrape down sides, if you need to.

2 • Pour about ¼ cup *batter** for each pancake onto a hot, lightly *greased** griddle. Cook pancakes over medium-high heat until tops are covered with bubbles and edges look a little dry; turn and cook other side. Serve warm with maple syrup. Makes 14 pancakes

FOR 1 PANCAKE: CALORIES 156 (43% from fat); FAT 7.4g (sat 1.5g, mono 2.6g, poly 2.5g); PROTEIN 4g; CARB 18.5g; FIBER 0.5g; CHOL 35mg; IRON 1.1mg; SODIUM 352mg; CALC 72mg

Bacon and Cheddar Perfect Pancakes:

• Cook, cool, and crumble 6 slices of bacon. Add crumbled bacon and 1 cup shredded sharp Cheddar cheese to pancake batter before cooking pancakes. Makes 20 pancakes

FOR 1 PANCAKE: CALORIES 141 (50% from fat); FAT 7.8g (sat 2.5g, mono 2.2g, poly 1.8g); PROTEIN 4.7g; CARB 13.2g; FIBER 0.4g; CHOL 32mg; IRON 0.8mg; SODIUM 326mg; CALC 90mg

Perfect Waffles:

• Cook pancake batter in a preheated, oiled waffle iron until golden. Makes 14 (4-inch) waffles

FOR 1 WAFFLE: CALORIES 156 (43% from fat); FAT 7.4g (sat 1.5g, mono 2.6g, poly 2.5g); PROTEIN 4g; CARB 18.5g; FIBER 0.5g; CHOL 35mg; IRON 1.1mg; SODIUM 352mg; CALC 72mg

* see glossary

Tip: Top Perfect Waffles with pineapple tidbits, banana slices, and chocolate syrup for a breakfast treat similar to a banana split.

CITRUSY FRENCH TOAST

To keep the cooked French toast slices warm while you're making more, place them on a baking sheet in a 300° oven. That way everyone can sit down and eat breakfast at the same time.

1 cup **complete pancake mix** (we used Aunt Jemima)

1 cup **water**

2 teaspoons grated **orange** rind

2 teaspoons grated **lemon** rind

2 tablespoons **powdered sugar**

¼ cup **butter or margarine**

8 slices **white sandwich bread**

1 • *Whisk** first 5 ingredients in a medium bowl until smooth.

2 • *Melt** 1 tablespoon butter in a big skillet over medium heat.
  • Dip 2 bread slices in *batter**, coating well. Cook 1 to 2 minutes on each side or until golden brown, turning toast with a spatula. Remove from pan; keep warm.
  • Do the same thing all over again with remaining butter, batter, and bread slices. Serve warm with maple syrup. Makes 4 servings

FOR 1 SERVING: CALORIES 458 (30% from fat); FAT 15.5g (sat 7.2g, mono 2.9g, poly 0.4g); PROTEIN 13.9g; CARB 68.4g; FIBER 1g; CHOL 34mg; IRON 2.8mg; SODIUM 957mg; CALC 200mg

* see glossary

LEMON-RAISIN DROP SCONES

Scones are sort of like biscuits, only sweeter. For this recipe, drop the dough onto the baking sheet just as if you were making chocolate chip cookies.

2 cups **all-purpose flour**

½ cup **sugar**

2 teaspoons **cream of tartar**

1 teaspoon **baking soda**

¼ teaspoon **salt**

1 teaspoon grated **lemon rind**

½ cup **butter or margarine**

½ cup **golden raisins**

⅔ cup **buttermilk**

1 • *Preheat** oven to 450°.

2 • *Stir** together first 6 ingredients in a medium bowl. Cut in butter with a pastry blender until crumbly.
• Add raisins and buttermilk, stirring just until dry ingredients are moistened.
• Drop dough evenly into 12 mounds on an ungreased baking sheet.

3 • *Bake** at 450° for 10 minutes or until golden. Remove baking sheet from the oven using oven mitts. Cool.
• Store scones in an airtight container up to 1 week. Makes 1 dozen scones

FOR 1 SCONE: CALORIES 203 (37% from fat); FAT 8.3g (sat 5.1g, mono 2g, poly 0.4g); PROTEIN 2.9g; CARB 30g; FIBER 0.8g; CHOL 22mg; IRON 1.1mg; SODIUM 225mg; CALC 9mg

* see glossary

CINNAMON RAISIN BREAD

"I made this recipe with my mom. It smells really good and tastes wonderful with extra raisins!" —Luke, Age 7

1 (¼-ounce) **envelope active dry yeast**

Pinch of **sugar**

1 cup warm **water** (100° to 110°)

2 tablespoons **canola oil**

2½ to 2¾ cups **bread flour**

3 tablespoons **sugar**

1 teaspoon **salt**

1 teaspoon **ground cinnamon**

½ cup **raisins**

Did you know?

A knife with teeth or a scalloped cutting edge is called a serrated knife. It's what you'll want to use when cutting something that's tougher on the outside than it is on the inside—like bread or tomatoes. The best way to use it is with a sawing motion.

1 Make the dough:
- Stir* together yeast*, a pinch* of sugar, and warm water in a 2-cup glass measuring cup. Let stand 5 minutes. Stir in oil.
- Stir together 1½ cups flour, 3 tablespoons sugar, salt, and cinnamon in a big bowl. Stir in yeast mixture and raisins. Stir in enough of the remaining flour to make a soft dough, probably about 1 cup.

2 Knead and shape the dough:
- Turn dough out onto a floured surface, and knead* 8 minutes or until smooth and elastic, adding small amounts of remaining flour to keep dough from sticking.
- Shape dough into a loaf, and place in a lightly greased* 8- x 4-inch loafpan. Let rise* in a warm place (85°), free from drafts, for 45 minutes or until doubled in size.

3
- Preheat* oven to 375°.

4
- Bake* at 375° for 25 minutes or until loaf is golden and sounds hollow when you thump the top with your finger. Remove loafpan from the oven using oven mitts. Invert* loaf onto a rack, and cool completely.
- Store bread in an airtight plastic bag up to 1 week. Makes 1 loaf

FOR 1 (½-INCH) SLICE: CALORIES 117 (17% from fat); FAT 2.2g (sat 0.2g, mono 1.1g, poly 0.7g); PROTEIN 2.9g; CARB 21.8g; FIBER 0.9g; CHOL 0mg; IRON 1.2mg; SODIUM 147mg; CALC 8mg

* see glossary

Note: It's easy to turn Cinnamon Raisin Bread dough into Beary Good Rolls. The instructions are on page 173.

**Prep: 15 min.
Cook: 15 min.**

ELEPHANT EARS

MAKE-AHEAD

These flaky pastries are known in Europe as palmiers (pahlm-YAYS), but a lot of people call them elephant ears because they think that's what they look like. What do you think?

1 (17¼-ounce) **package frozen puff pastry,** thawed

3 tablespoons **butter or margarine,** melted

¼ cup grated **Parmesan cheese**

2 teaspoons **paprika**

½ teaspoon **pepper**

1 **egg** yolk

1 tablespoon **water**

1 • *Preheat** oven to 375°.

2 • *Roll** 1 pastry sheet into a 13- x 11-inch rectangle. *Drizzle** half of butter over pastry, and *spread** it out using a pastry brush. Sprinkle with half of cheese, paprika, and pepper.
  • Roll up both short sides of pastry, like a jelly-roll cake, ending at the middle of pastry sheet where the two rolls will meet and touch.
  • Do the same thing all over again with remaining pastry sheet, butter, cheese, paprika, and pepper.

3 • Cut rolls crosswise into ⅓-inch-thick slices. Place on lightly *greased** baking sheets.
  • *Whisk** egg yolk and 1 tablespoon water in a small bowl. Brush egg mixture evenly over pastries using a pastry brush. *Bake** at 375° for 10 to 15 minutes or until golden brown.
  • Remove baking sheets from the oven using oven mitts. Cool.
  • Store in an airtight container up to 1 week. Makes 5½ dozen elephant ears

FOR 1 ELEPHANT EAR: CALORIES 48 (66% from fat); FAT 3.5g (sat 1.1g, mono 1.8g, poly 0.4g); PROTEIN 0.7g; CARB 3.4g; FIBER 0.1g; CHOL 5mg; IRON 0.2mg; SODIUM 45mg; CALC 5mg

* see glossary

44 BREADS

Prep: 15 min.
Cook: 20 min.
Other: 5 min.

EASY SPOON ROLLS

Self-rising flour makes these rolls puff up without adding any other leavening ingredients. Yeast makes breads puff up, too, but in this recipe it simply adds flavor.

1 (¼-ounce) **envelope active dry yeast**

¼ cup **sugar**

2 cups warm **water** (100° to 110°)

4 cups **self-rising flour**

¾ cup **butter or margarine,** melted and cooled

1 **large egg,** lightly beaten

1 • *Preheat** oven to 400°.

2 • *Stir** together *yeast**, a *pinch** of sugar, and warm water in a big bowl; let stand 5 minutes.
   • Add remaining sugar, flour, butter, and egg to yeast mixture. Stir with a wooden spoon until blended. Spoon *batter** into *greased** muffin pans, filling two-thirds full.

3 • *Bake** at 400° for 20 minutes or until rolls are golden. Remove muffin pans from the oven using oven mitts. *Invert** rolls onto a wire rack. Serve warm. Makes 2 dozen rolls

FOR 1 ROLL: CALORIES 136 (40% from fat); FAT 6.1g (sat 3.7g, mono 1.6g, poly 0.3g); PROTEIN 2.5g; CARB 17.7g; FIBER 0.6g; CHOL 24mg; IRON 1.1mg; SODIUM 308mg; CALC 73mg

* see glossary

**Prep: 5 min.
Cook: 25 min.**

CORNY MUFFINS

Using cupcake liners makes these muffins easily fall out and clean-up a cinch.

2 cups **yellow or white cornmeal mix**

¾ cup **all-purpose flour**

1 tablespoon **sugar**

2 **large eggs,** lightly beaten

2 cups **buttermilk**

¼ cup **butter or margarine,** melted

1 • *Preheat** oven to 425°.

2 • *Stir** together first 3 ingredients in a big bowl; make a *well** in the center of mixture using a wooden spoon.
• *Whisk** eggs, buttermilk, and butter in a small bowl until smooth. Pour buttermilk mixture into well, and stir just until moistened. Spoon *batter** into lightly *greased** muffin pans or muffin pans lined with cupcake liners, filling three-fourths full.

3 • *Bake** at 425° for 25 minutes or until golden. Remove muffin pans from the oven using oven mitts. *Invert** muffins onto a wire rack. Serve warm. Makes 16 muffins

FOR 1 MUFFIN: CALORIES 133 (32% from fat); FAT 4.8g (sat 2.7g, mono 1.1g, poly 0.4g); PROTEIN 3.7g; CARB 19.4g; FIBER 1g; CHOL 38mg; IRON 1.5mg; SODIUM 278mg; CALC 55mg

* see glossary

Prep: 15 min.
Cook: 24 min.

STRAWBERRY FRENCH TOASTWICHES

"The powdered sugar is fun to sprinkle, tastes great, and is super soft. I'm going to make this for Nana when she comes to visit next." —Sarah, Age 9

¹/₃ cup **tub-style cream cheese**

12 **slices white bread**

6 tablespoons **strawberry preserves**

3 **large eggs**

3 tablespoons **milk**

¹/₈ teaspoon **salt**

Vegetable cooking spray

Powdered sugar (optional)

Fresh strawberries (optional)

1 • *Spread** cream cheese evenly over 1 side of 6 bread slices. Spread 1 tablespoon preserves evenly over cream cheese; top with remaining bread slices.

2 • *Whisk** eggs, milk, and salt in a shallow dish.

3 Cook the Toastwiches:
- Spray a big nonstick skillet with vegetable cooking spray, and place over medium heat until hot.
- Dip 1 sandwich into egg mixture, coating both sides. Cook sandwich 1 to 2 minutes on each side or until golden brown.
- Do the same thing all over again with the remaining sandwiches and egg mixture. Sprinkle with powdered sugar, and serve with strawberries, if you'd like. Serve warm. Makes 6 sandwiches

FOR 1 SANDWICH: CALORIES 356 (26% from fat); FAT 10.2g (sat 3.8g, mono 2.3g, poly 0.5g); PROTEIN 14.4g; CARB 53.9g; FIBER 0g; CHOL 121mg; IRON 2.1mg; SODIUM 645mg; CALC 112mg

* see glossary

GOOD MORNING STICKY BUNS

This ooey-gooey breakfast bread is convenient for weekends and special holidays because you make it at night and bake it in the morning.

2 teaspoons **butter or margarine**, softened

½ cup **chopped pecans or walnuts**

1 (25-ounce) **package frozen roll dough,** thawed

1 (3.4-ounce) **package butterscotch instant pudding mix**

½ cup **butter or margarine,** melted

½ cup firmly packed **brown sugar**

¾ teaspoon **ground cinnamon**

1 • *Spread** 2 teaspoons butter over the inside of a 10-inch Bundt pan. Sprinkle pecans in the bottom of the pan. Arrange dough in pan over pecans. Sprinkle pudding mix over dough.
• *Stir** together melted butter, brown sugar, and cinnamon; pour over dough. Cover and *chill** in the refrigerator 8 hours.

2 • *Preheat** oven to 350°.

3 • *Bake** at 350° for 30 minutes or until golden brown.
• Remove pan from the oven using oven mitts. Carefully *invert** onto a serving plate. Serve warm. Makes 8 servings

FOR 1 SERVING: CALORIES 505 (40% from fat); FAT 22.3g (sat 10.6g, mono 6.2g, poly 2.1g); PROTEIN 7g; CARB 70.8g; FIBER 2.4g; CHOL 33mg; IRON 2.8mg; SODIUM 716mg; CALC 54mg

* see glossary

Prep: 20 min.
Cook: 30 min.
Other: 10 min.

CaN-CaN BROWN BREaD

Recycled vegetable cans make perfect baking containers and are inexpensive.

Vegetable cooking spray
½ cup **whole wheat flour**
½ cup **all-purpose flour**
½ cup **yellow cornmeal**
½ teaspoon **baking soda**
½ teaspoon **salt**
¾ teaspoon **ground cinnamon**
1 cup **plain low-fat yogurt**
⅓ cup **molasses**
½ cup **raisins**

1 • *Preheat** oven to 350°. Prepare cans for baking bread as directed below. Spray the inside of each can with cooking spray.

2 • *Stir** together whole wheat flour and next 5 ingredients in a big bowl; make a *well** in center of mixture using a wooden spoon.
• *Whisk** yogurt and molasses in a small bowl until smooth. Pour yogurt mixture and raisins into well, and stir just until moistened. Spoon *batter** into prepared cans.

3 • *Bake** at 350° for 30 minutes or until a wooden pick inserted in center of each loaf comes out clean. Remove cans from the oven using oven mitts. Cool 10 minutes. Remove bread from cans, and cool completely on a wire rack. Makes 3 small loaves

FOR 1 (½-INCH) SLICE: CALORIES 60 (5% from fat); FAT 0.3g (sat 0.1g, mono 0g, poly 0.1g); PROTEIN 1.4g; CARB 13.3g; FIBER 0.7g; CHOL 1mg; IRON 0.7mg; SODIUM 122mg; CALC 38mg

* see glossary

Tip: Beans typically come in 16-ounce cans. To get the cans ready for this recipe, remove one end from three (16-ounce) cans, and use the contents as you like. Wash the cans in warm sudsy water, rinse, and dry. Be very careful doing this because the open end may have sharp edges.

Better-Than-The-Box
Mac and Cheese,
page 62

EGGS & CHEESE

Prep: 15 min.
Cook: 27 min., 30 sec.
Other: 35 min.

UP TO THE CHALLENGE?

GREEN CHILE-CHEESE STRATA

A strata is an egg and cheese casserole. This one would be just right to serve for brunch—that's the meal served late in the morning that takes the place of breakfast and lunch.

6 slices **firm white bread,** cut into 1-inch cubes

2 tablespoons **butter or margarine**

1 **small onion,** finely chopped

2 cups **milk**

3 **large eggs,** lightly beaten

½ teaspoon **salt**

⅛ teaspoon **ground red pepper** (optional)

⅛ teaspoon **ground cumin**

1 (4½-ounce) **can chopped green chiles**

2 cups (8 ounces) shredded **sharp Cheddar cheese**

1 • Arrange bread cubes in a single layer on a baking sheet. Let sit at *room temperature** 30 minutes or until bread dries out slightly.

2 • *Preheat** oven to 350°.

3 • Place butter in a big microwave-safe bowl. Cover with a paper towel, and microwave at HIGH 30 seconds or until butter melts. *Stir** in onion. Cover and microwave at HIGH 2 more minutes or until onion is *tender**. Cool.
• Add milk, eggs, salt, red pepper, if you'd like, and cumin to onion mixture; *whisk** until blended. Stir in chiles and cheese. *Fold** bread cubes into milk mixture.
• Spoon bread mixture into 6 lightly *greased** (10-ounce) custard cups. Place custard cups on a jelly-roll pan.

4 • *Bake** at 350° for 25 minutes or until golden brown and puffed. Remove pan from the oven using oven mitts. Let sit 5 minutes.
Makes 6 servings

FOR 1 SERVING: CALORIES 384 (53% from fat); FAT 22.4g (sat 12.7g, mono 2.6g, poly 0.7g); PROTEIN 18.9g; CARB 27.1g; FIBER 0.9g; CHOL 157mg; IRON 1.2mg; SODIUM 867mg; CALC 444mg

* see glossary

Prep: 6 min.
Cook: 6 min.

SUPER-CREAMY SCRAMBLED EGGS

"I made this recipe when my friend came to visit. She was so impressed that I made the eggs myself. I doubled the recipe, and cooked it in a really big skillet so I got to crack a lot of eggs—that's my favorite part." —Sarah, Age 9

6 **large eggs**

1 tablespoon **Dijon mustard**

⅛ teaspoon **pepper**

1 (3-ounce) **package cream cheese,** cut into small cubes

1 tablespoon chopped **fresh chives** (optional)

1 tablespoon chopped **fresh parsley** (optional)

1 tablespoon **butter or margarine**

Salt (optional)

1 • *Whisk** together first 3 ingredients in a medium bowl. *Stir** in cream cheese and chives and parsley, if you'd like.

2 • *Melt** butter in an 8-inch nonstick skillet over medium heat, tilting pan to coat bottom; pour in egg mixture.

• Cook, without stirring, until mixture begins to *set** on bottom. Slowly drag a spatula across bottom of pan to form large pieces of cooked egg. Continue cooking until eggs are thickened and firm throughout, but still moist. (Do not stir constantly.) Sprinkle with salt, if you'd like. Makes 4 servings

FOR 1 SERVING: CALORIES 210 (76% from fat); FAT 17.7g (sat 8.8g, mono 5.7g, poly 1.4g); PROTEIN 11.1g; CARB 1.3g; FIBER 0.1g; CHOL 348mg; IRON 1.7mg; SODIUM 237mg; CALC 60mg

* see glossary

Note: Some of our kid tasters really liked the taste of chives and parsley, while some didn't. Would you add them or not?

Prep: 10 min.
Cook: 40 min.
Other: 8 hrs.

PUMPKIN PIE IN a CUP

This egg-rich recipe uses a *water bath*. As you can imagine, that means putting a container of food—or in this case custard cups—into another pan that's filled with warm water. The water surrounds the food with gentle heat as it cooks and keeps the eggs from overcooking.

4 large eggs

1 (15-ounce) **can pumpkin**

¾ cup **sugar**

1 teaspoon **ground cinnamon**

½ teaspoon **ground ginger**

½ teaspoon **salt**

½ teaspoon **ground nutmeg**

½ teaspoon **vanilla extract**

1 (12-ounce) **can evaporated milk**

Whipped topping (optional)

1 • *Preheat** oven to 350°.

2 • *Beat** eggs in a big bowl at medium speed with an electric mixer until blended. Add pumpkin and next 6 ingredients. Beat just until blended. *Stir** in milk.

3 • Pour pumpkin mixture into 8 ungreased (6-ounce) custard cups. Place cups in a big pan. Add hot water to pan to a depth of 1 inch.

4 • *Bake** at 350° for 40 minutes or until done or *set**. To test for doneness, carefully shake the pan using an oven mitt. The recipe is ready when the centers wiggle a little bit but aren't liquidy.

• Remove pan from the oven using oven mitts. Carefully remove cups from pan using oven mitts, too. Cool completely. Cover and *chill** in the refrigerator at least 8 hours or up to 3 days.

• Top each serving with whipped topping, if you'd like. Makes 8 servings

FOR 1 SERVING: CALORIES 130 (19% from fat); FAT 2.7g (sat 0.9g, mono 1g, poly 0.4g); PROTEIN 3.8g; CARB 23.7g; FIBER 1.7g; CHOL 106mg; IRON 1.3mg; SODIUM 183mg; CALC 31mg

* see glossary

Did you know

An electric mixer makes foods creamy and smooth with little effort. But it's a powerful kitchen appliance and needs to be used properly to prevent accidents. Here are some safety tips:
• Always have a grown-up present.
• Always unplug the mixer to attach and remove the beaters.
• Pull back your hair in a ponytail if it's long, and don't wear long necklaces while using a mixer.
• Never—ever! touch the beaters while the mixer is running.

DUTCH BABY

BREAKFAST BOOSTER

UP TO THE CHALLENGE?

You'll want to leave the oven light on and watch as this baby bakes. The batter will puff up like a balloon and turn brown. Don't open the door, because if you do, the puff will deflate too early. When it's done and out of the oven, it will deflate, forming a big edible bowl perfect for filling with sweetened fruit.

1 pint **fresh strawberries,** sliced

1 pint **fresh blueberries**

2 tablespoons **granulated sugar**

½ cup **bread flour**

¼ teaspoon **salt**

½ cup **milk**

2 **large eggs**

1 tablespoon **butter or margarine**

Powdered sugar (optional)

1 • *Preheat** oven to 450°.

2 • *Stir** together first 3 ingredients in a medium bowl; set aside.

3 • Combine flour, salt, milk, and eggs in the container of an electric blender. Top with cover, and process 1 minute. Set *batter** aside.

4 • Place a 10-inch ovenproof nonstick skillet in the oven 5 minutes to preheat.
 • Remove hot skillet from the oven using oven mitts, and place on a heat-proof surface. Add butter to hot skillet, and carefully swirl to coat skillet. Pour batter into skillet.
 • *Bake** at 450° for 10 minutes. Reduce heat to 350°, and bake 10 more minutes or until puffed and brown.

5 • Remove skillet from the oven using oven mitts. **ⓐ** Cool slightly. Fill with fruit mixture, and sprinkle with powdered sugar, if you'd like. **Ⓑ** Cut into wedges to serve. Makes 4 servings

FOR 1 SERVING: CALORIES 234 (27% from fat); FAT 7.1g (sat 3.2g, mono 2g, poly 0.9g); PROTEIN 7.3g; CARB 37.1g; FIBER 3.8g; CHOL 116mg; IRON 1.8mg; SODIUM 215mg; CALC 69mg

* see glossary

**Prep: 12 min.
Cook: 30 min.**

BETTER-THAN-THE-BOX MAC AND CHEESE

"Cooking is awesome when your family and friends love your recipes." —Taylor, Age 11

12 ounces uncooked **elbow macaroni**

¼ cup **butter or margarine**

2 tablespoons **all-purpose flour**

1½ cups **milk**

1 (8-ounce) **loaf pasteurized prepared cheese product** (we used Velveeta), cubed

Dash of **garlic powder**

Dash of **pepper**

2½ cups (10 ounces) shredded **sharp Cheddar cheese** (we used Cracker Barrel)

3 tablespoons grated **Parmesan cheese**

1 • *Preheat** oven to 350°.

2 • Cook macaroni in boiling water according to package directions; *drain** macaroni in a colander, and set aside.

3 • *Melt** butter in a Dutch oven over low heat. *Whisk** in flour until smooth. Cook, whisking constantly, 1 minute.
 • Gradually add milk; cook over medium heat, whisking constantly, 6 minutes or until mixture is thickened and bubbly.
 • *Stir** in cubed cheese, garlic powder, and pepper. Reduce heat, and stir just until cheese melts. Stir in cooked macaroni.

4 • Spoon half of macaroni mixture in a lightly *greased** 11- x 7-inch baking dish; sprinkle with half of Cheddar cheese. Do the same thing all over again with remaining macaroni mixture and Cheddar cheese. Top with Parmesan cheese.
 • *Bake** at 350° for 20 minutes or until hot and bubbly. Remove dish from the oven using oven mitts. Makes 6 servings

FOR 1 SERVING: CALORIES 610 (51% from fat); FAT 34.3g (sat 21.9g, mono 2.8g, poly 0.8g); PROTEIN 27.1g; CARB 49.4g; FIBER 1.9g; CHOL 97mg; IRON 2.1mg; SODIUM 1,249mg; CALC 623mg

* see glossary

Note: For individual servings, layer the macaroni mixture, Cheddar cheese, and Parmesan cheese in 6 (8-ounce) ovenproof ramekins, and bake for 15 minutes or until hot and bubbly.

GRILLED HAM 'N' CHEESE

This sandwich rocks as the ultimate grilled cheese. Let it stand a few minutes before you cut it in half so the cheese won't ooze out too much.

1 cup (4 ounces) shredded **Monterey Jack cheese**

1 cup (4 ounces) shredded **Cheddar cheese**

2 tablespoons **mayonnaise**

1 tablespoon **prepared mustard**

1 **green onion,** finely chopped

8 slices **white or wheat sandwich bread**

4 ounces **thinly sliced ham**

Vegetable cooking spray

1
- *Stir** together first 5 ingredients in a small bowl. *Spread** cheese mixture evenly on 1 side of 4 bread slices. Top with ham and remaining bread slices.
- *Preheat** griddle to medium-high.

2
- Coat both sides of sandwiches with cooking spray, and place on hot griddle. Cook over medium-high heat about 3 minutes or until bread is browned. Turn and brown other side of sandwiches. Makes 4 servings

FOR 1 SERVING: CALORIES 516 (47% from fat); FAT 27g (sat 11.8g, mono 2.8g, poly 0.6g); PROTEIN 28.1g; CARB 41.8g; FIBER 0.1g; CHOL 71mg; IRON 2.1mg; SODIUM 1,294mg; CALC 486mg

* see glossary

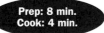

**Prep: 8 min.
Cook: 4 min.**

TOASTY FRUIT AND CHEESE SANDWICHES

"I would have never thought of eating all these ingredients together in a sandwich but it was yummy. Next time I'll try it with strawberries instead of apples." —Hope, Age 7

1 **medium apple**, cored and thinly sliced

2 tablespoons **orange juice**

8 slices **raisin bread**

½ (8-ounce) **package cream cheese**, softened

2 tablespoons **raisins**

1 tablespoon **orange marmalade**

⅛ teaspoon **ground cinnamon**

1 • Place apple slices in a small bowl. *Drizzle** orange juice over apple slices; *toss** to coat.

2 • Toast raisin bread in toaster.

3 • *Stir** together cream cheese and next 3 ingredients in a small bowl. *Spread** cream cheese mixture evenly on 1 side of 4 slices of toast. Top each with 3 apple slices and remaining slices of toast. Makes 4 servings

FOR 1 SERVING: CALORIES 299 (37% from fat); FAT 12.3g (sat 6.8g, mono 4g, poly 0.8g); PROTEIN 6.6g; CARB 43.1g; FIBER 3.8g; CHOL 31mg; IRON 2.1mg; SODIUM 291mg; CALC 66mg

* see glossary

HEAVENLY DEVILED EGGS

Here's a fun way to fill Heavenly Deviled Eggs: Spoon the yolk mixture into a small zip-top freezer bag, and seal it. Cut a small opening in the bottom corner, and gently squirt the yolk mixture into the egg whites. Sprinkling paprika over the Deviled Eggs makes them taste no different. Our kid testers preferred it because it made them more colorful.

6 **large eggs**

2 tablespoons **mayonnaise**

1½ tablespoons **sweet pickle relish**

1 teaspoon **prepared mustard**

⅛ teaspoon **salt**

Dash of **pepper**

Paprika (optional)

1 • Place eggs in a single layer in a saucepan; add water to measure at least 1 inch above eggs. Bring to a *boil** over high heat; cover, remove from heat, and let sit 15 minutes.

2 • Pour off water. Fill the saucepan with cold water, and let it sit until completely cool. Crack hard-cooked eggs, and remove shells. Hold each egg under a small stream of cold running water as you peel off shell.

3 • Slice eggs in half lengthwise, and carefully remove yolks. Place yolks and mayonnaise on a small plate; *mash** with a dinner fork until blended. *Stir** in relish, mustard, salt, and pepper. Spoon yolk mixture into egg whites. Sprinkle with paprika, if you'd like. Cover and *chill** in the refrigerator at least 1 hour or up to 3 days. Makes 1 dozen deviled eggs

FOR 1 DEVILED EGG: CALORIES 56 (71% from fat); FAT 4.9g (sat 1g, mono 1g, poly 0.4g); PROTEIN 3.2g; CARB 0.6g; FIBER 0g; CHOL 107mg; IRON 0.5mg; SODIUM 86mg; CALC 13mg

* see glossary

Tip: There are a couple of ways to crack hard-cooked eggs. You can tap each egg with the back of a spoon until cracks form all over the shell. Gently tapping each egg firmly on a counter works just as well. Also, you can put all the eggs in a saucepan, cover the pan, and then shake it vigorously so that the eggs crack from bumping into one another. When you're done with cracking, gently roll each egg between your hands to loosen the shell. Then hold it under a small stream of running water, and peel the shell away with your fingers.

QUICK PiZZa DiP

"I did this recipe by myself without help from Mom or Dad. It was a blast to make, especially since everyone loved eating it, even my little brother! I hope to serve it at my next slumber party." —Taylor, Age 11

1 (8-ounce) **package cream cheese**, softened

1 teaspoon **dried Italian seasoning**

1 (14-ounce) **jar pizza sauce**

1 (3-ounce) **package sliced pepperoni**, chopped

1 (2¼-ounce) **can sliced ripe olives**, drained

1 **small green bell pepper**, chopped (optional)

¼ cup minced **onion** (optional)

½ cup (2 ounces) shredded **mozzarella cheese**

½ cup shredded **Parmesan cheese**

1
• *Stir** together cream cheese and dried Italian seasoning in a small bowl; *spread** into a lightly *greased** 9-inch microwave-safe pieplate.
• Spread pizza sauce over cream cheese mixture; top with pepperoni and olives. Add bell pepper and onion, if you'd like. Sprinkle with mozzarella and Parmesan cheeses.

2
• Microwave at HIGH 2 to 3 minutes or until thoroughly heated. Serve pizza dip with soft breadsticks. Makes 4 cups dip

FOR ¼ CUP: CALORIES 108 (66% from fat); FAT 7.9g (sat 4.4g, mono 2.8g, poly 0.4g); PROTEIN 4.2g; CARB 5.2g; FIBER 0.9g; CHOL 24mg; IRON 0.5mg; SODIUM 352mg; CALC 71mg

* see glossary

Make-Ahead Tip: Prepare recipe through step 1, and cover with plastic wrap. Refrigerate overnight. Uncover and microwave at HIGH 4 to 5 minutes or until thoroughly heated.

Did you know?

A microwave oven cooks by using radio waves. These waves cause the tiny molecules in food to vibrate so quickly that enough friction and heat are created to cook it.

BaCoN-CHEESE CUPS

"Pressing microwave buttons is fun but having to wait on the bacon to cook isn't. See, I love, love, love bacon. I'd like this recipe better with a whole pack of bacon!" —Elizabeth, Age 7

2 (3-ounce) **packages cream cheese**, softened

1 **large egg**

2 tablespoons **milk**

½ cup (2 ounces) shredded **Swiss cheese**

1 **green onion**, chopped

1 (12-ounce) **package refrigerated flaky biscuits** (we used Pillsbury Golden Layer)

5 **bacon slices**, cooked and crumbled

1 • *Preheat** oven to 375°.

2 • *Beat** cream cheese, egg, and milk in a medium bowl at medium speed with an electric mixture until blended. *Stir** in shredded Swiss cheese and chopped green onions.

3 • Separate biscuits. Pat 1 biscuit into a 5-inch circle, and press into the bottom and up sides of a *greased** muffin cup. Sprinkle about 1 teaspoon crumbled bacon into biscuit shell, and top with 2 tablespoons cream cheese mixture. Sprinkle with 1 teaspoon crumbled bacon. Do the same thing all over again with remaining biscuits, bacon, and cream cheese mixture.

4 • *Bake** at 375° for 22 minutes or until *set**. Remove muffin pan from the oven using oven mitts. Cool completely on a wire rack. Makes 10 servings

FOR 1 SERVING: CALORIES 218 (60% from fat); FAT 14.5g (sat 6.9g, mono 2.5g, poly 0.4g); PROTEIN 6.6g; CARB 15g; FIBER 0g; CHOL 49mg; IRON 1.1mg; SODIUM 494mg; CALC 91mg

* see glossary

Did you know?

Cheesemakers call the holes in Swiss cheese "eyes." The longer the cheese ages the bigger the eyes get and the stronger the flavor becomes. It can take as little as 2 months to as much as 2 years to make Swiss cheese.

Chicken Salad
Scoops, page 82

EXTRA EASY LASAGNA

When the lasagna is done it will be bubbly, hot, and super juicy. Letting it sit at room temperature allows it to cool enough to eat and for the pasta to absorb the extra juices. Why not use that time to set the table?

1 pound **ground round**

4 cups **tomato-basil pasta sauce** (we used Classico)

6 uncooked **lasagna noodles**

1 (15-ounce) **container ricotta cheese**

2 cups (8 ounces) shredded **mozzarella cheese**

¼ cup hot **water**

1 • *Preheat** oven to 375°.

2 • Cook ground round in a big skillet over medium heat, stirring until it crumbles and is no longer pink; *drain**. *Stir** in pasta sauce.

3 • *Spread** one-third meat sauce in a lightly *greased** 12- x 8-inch baking dish. Arrange 3 uncooked noodles over sauce. Spread half of ricotta cheese over noodles; sprinkle with one-third of mozzarella cheese. Do the same thing all over again with half of remaining meat sauce, remaining noodles, remaining ricotta, and half of remaining mozzarella cheese. Top with remaining meat sauce and mozzarella cheese.

• Carefully pour ¼ cup hot water around inside edge of dish. Tightly cover with 2 layers of aluminum foil.

4 • *Bake** at 375° for 45 minutes. Uncover and bake 10 more minutes. Remove baking dish from the oven using oven mitts. Let stand 10 minutes before serving. Makes 6 servings

FOR 1 SERVING: CALORIES 519 (45% from fat); FAT 26.2g (sat 13.5g, mono 3.3g, poly 0.3g); PROTEIN 39.7g; CARB 35g; FIBER 3.4g; CHOL 97mg; IRON 3.4mg; SODIUM 899mg; CALC 668mg

* see glossary

Prep: 7 min.
Cook: 14 min.

PEANUTTY CHICKEN AND PASTA

The twists and turns of corkscrew pasta are ideal for trapping the peanutty sauce. Macaroni works well, too.

¼ cup **low-sodium soy sauce**

2 tablespoons **coconut milk**

2 tablespoons **creamy peanut butter**

¼ teaspoon **dark sesame oil**

8 ounces uncooked **corkscrew pasta**

2 cups chopped **cooked chicken breast**

½ cup **preshredded carrot**

2 **green onions,** thinly sliced

¼ cup chopped **red bell pepper**

⅓ cup chopped **unsalted peanuts**

1 • *Whisk** together first 4 ingredients in a small bowl; set sauce aside.

2 • Cook pasta according to package directions, omitting salt and fat. *Drain** and place in a big bowl. Add sauce, chicken, carrot, green onions, and bell pepper; *toss** gently to blend. Sprinkle with chopped peanuts. Makes 4 servings

FOR 1 SERVING: CALORIES 453 (28% from fat); FAT 13.9g (sat 2.5g, mono 4.1g, poly 3g); PROTEIN 34.6g; CARB 47.1g; FIBER 4g; CHOL 60mg; IRON 3.3mg; SODIUM 711mg; CALC 39mg

* see glossary

Tip: Refrigerate leftovers in an airtight container. Reheat it, if you'd like, in the microwave, or skip reheating and serve it cold like a pasta salad.

Did you know?

Washing your hands is the best way to stop germs from making you or someone else sick. It's especially important before you cook or eat food that you touch with your hands. The next time you scrub up, remember these hand-washing hints:
• Use warm water (not cold or hot) when you wash your hands.
• Work up a sudsy lather with soap on both sides of your hands, your wrists, and between your fingers. And don't forget to wash around your nails; this is one place germs like to hide.
• Wash for about 10 to 15 seconds. That's about how long it takes to sing "Happy Birthday to You" nice and slow.
• Rinse and dry well with a clean towel.

BEGINNER'S POT ROAST

A Dutch oven and its tight-fitting lid make a chamber for the ingredients that seals in the delicious juices. When the pot roast is done, you'll discover those juices transformed into a rich gravy perfect for spooning over mashed potatoes.

1 (3- to 4-pound) **eye of round roast**

1 **large sweet onion,** sliced

1 (10¾-ounce) **can cream of mushroom soup**

½ cup **water**

1 (1.12-ounce) **package brown gravy mix** (we used Knorr Classic)

1 **garlic clove,** minced

1 • *Preheat** oven to 325°.

2 • Place roast in a lightly *greased** Dutch oven, and top with sliced onion. *Stir** together soup, water, gravy mix, and garlic; pour over roast.

3 • Cover with Dutch oven lid, and *bake** at 325° for 3 hours and 30 minutes or until *tender**. Remove Dutch oven from the oven using oven mitts. Let stand 10 minutes before serving. Makes 8 to 10 servings

FOR 1 SERVING: CALORIES 305 (39% from fat); FAT 13.3g (sat 4.6g, mono 4.6g, poly 0.7g); PROTEIN 37g; CARB 7.1g; FIBER 0.7g; CHOL 91mg; IRON 2.6mg; SODIUM 524mg; CALC 13mg

* see glossary

Tip: This is a terrific make-ahead dish. After baking, cool the roast completely, and remove it from the Dutch oven, reserving the gravy. Cut the roast into ¼-inch-thick slices, and arrange in a lightly greased 13- x 9-inch baking dish. Pour the gravy over the sliced roast. Cover tightly with aluminum foil, and refrigerate up to 3 days. Reheat (covered with foil) in a 325° oven for 30 minutes or until thoroughly heated.

EL PASO OVEN-FRIED CHICKEN

This crunchy chicken tastes great by itself. But if you want to dip it, our kid testers suggest salsa and Ranch dressing.

1 (10-ounce) **bag chili-cheese flavored corn chips,** finely crushed (about 2½ cups crushed)

2 pounds **chicken tenders**

⅓ cup **reduced-fat mayonnaise**

Vegetable cooking spray

1 • *Preheat** oven to 450°.

2 • Carefully open bag of corn chips just enough to release the airtight seal. Roll down the top of the package, pressing extra air out of bag; seal bag with a chip clip or clothes pin. Finely crush corn chips in bag using a rolling pin. Pour crushed corn chips into a shallow dish.

3 • Pat chicken dry with a paper towel, and brush with mayonnaise on all sides. *Dredge** chicken in crushed corn chips; lightly spray with cooking spray. (Throw away any leftover crushed corn chips.)

4 • Place a big baking sheet in a 450° oven for 5 minutes to preheat.
• Remove hot baking sheet from the oven using oven mitts. Carefully place chicken on hot pan.
• *Bake** at 450° for 18 to 20 minutes or until crust is lightly browned. Remove baking sheet from the oven using oven mitts. Makes 8 servings

FOR 1 SERVING: CALORIES 324 (39% from fat); FAT 14.1g (sat 2.4g, mono 0.3g, poly 0.3g); PROTEIN 28.5g; CARB 18.4g; FIBER 1.1g; CHOL 66mg; IRON 0.8mg; SODIUM 457mg; CALC 58mg

* see glossary

CHiCKEN SaLaD SCooPS

SUPERFAST & EASY

NO COOK

JUST FOR FUN

Ice cream cones that aren't sweet—ironically called "cake" cones—make fun, edible serving containers for this simple chicken salad. Fill them just before you plan to eat so the cones will stay crisp.

1 (9.75-ounce) **can chunk breast of chicken,** drained

½ cup finely chopped **celery**

¼ cup shredded **carrots**

¼ cup **raisins**

¼ cup **dry-roasted peanuts,** chopped

½ cup **reduced-fat mayonnaise**

4 **cake ice cream cones**

Curly leaf lettuce (optional)

1 • Combine first 5 ingredients in a medium bowl. Add mayonnaise to chicken mixture, stirring gently until combined. Cover with plastic wrap, and *chill** chicken salad in the refrigerator at least 1 hour.

2 • Just before serving, line cones with lettuce leaves, if you'd like; fill with chicken salad. Makes 4 servings

FOR 1 SERVING: CALORIES 195 (45% from fat); FAT 9.8g (sat 1.7g, mono 2.3 g, poly 1.6g); PROTEIN 11.5g; CARB 17.4g; FIBER 1.6g; CHOL 30mg; IRON 0.6mg; SODIUM 497mg; CALC 19mg

* see glossary

Note: Substitute 1 cup chopped cooked chicken for canned, if you'd like.

Did you know?

Cake cones are baked from batter poured into molds. The first molded cones had pointed bottoms, but the most common molded cones now have flat bottoms. The little ribs on the outside of the cake cones make them stronger so they won't break when they're filled with ice cream...or chicken salad!

SHRIMP AND RED PEPPER PASTA

"This meal has all my favorites in it—Ranch dressing, cheese, and shrimp! I thought it was going to take a long time to peel the shrimp but my mom and I did it in just a few minutes and we weren't even racing." —David, Age 10

8 ounces uncooked **angel hair pasta**

⅓ cup **Ranch dressing**

1 (5-ounce) **package refrigerated shredded Parmesan cheese**

2 tablespoons **butter or margarine**

1⅓ pounds **unpeeled medium-size shrimp,** peeled and deveined

½ pound sliced **fresh mushrooms**

1 (12-ounce) **jar roasted red peppers,** drained and cut into strips

½ cup chopped **fresh basil**

¼ teaspoon **black pepper**

1 • Cook pasta according to package directions, omitting salt; *drain** and set aside.

2 • *Stir** together dressing and cheese in a big bowl; set aside.

3 • While pasta cooks, *melt** butter in a big skillet over medium-high heat. Add shrimp; cook 3 to 5 minutes or until shrimp turn pink, stirring often. Remove shrimp from skillet using a slotted spoon, and add to salad dressing mixture.

• Return skillet to medium-high heat; add mushrooms, and *sauté** 2 minutes or until mushrooms are *tender**. Remove mushrooms from skillet using a slotted spoon, and add to salad dressing mixture.

4 • Add pasta, red peppers, basil, and black pepper to salad dressing mixture; *toss** gently. Serve hot. Makes 4 servings

FOR 1 SERVING: CALORIES 687 (39% from fat); FAT 29.9g (sat 12.1g, mono 5.2g, poly 2.4g); PROTEIN 53.8g; CARB 49.7g; FIBER 2.8g; CHOL 275mg; IRON 6.1mg; SODIUM 1,295mg; CALC 552mg

* see glossary

Tip: Look for "easy peel" shrimp in your grocer's freezer section. The shrimp shells have been pre-cut so it's really easy to slip off the peel and rinse away the vein under cool running water.

THAi CHICKEN WRAPS

If you're an adventurous eater, you'll love this cool Asian sandwich. Ordinary peanut butter and jelly—actually preserves—are star ingredients.

3 (4-ounce) **skinless, boneless chicken breasts**

7 tablespoons **sesame ginger 30-minute marinade** (we used Lawry's)

2 teaspoons **vegetable oil**

¼ cup **creamy peanut butter**

4 (8-inch) **98% fat-free whole wheat flour tortillas**

¼ cup **pineapple preserves**

1⅓ cups shredded **iceberg lettuce**

1 **green onion,** thinly sliced

1 • Place chicken in a zip-top freezer bag; add 4 tablespoons marinade. Seal bag, and turn to coat chicken. *Marinate** in refrigerator 30 minutes.

2 Prepare the chicken:
 • Remove chicken from bag, discarding marinade.
 • Cook chicken in hot oil in a big nonstick skillet over medium-high heat 6 minutes on each side or until done. Remove from skillet, and let cool slightly. Cut each chicken breast diagonally into ¼-inch-thick slices.

3 • *Stir** together peanut butter and remaining 3 tablespoons marinade in a small bowl.

4 Assemble the wraps:
 • *Spread** 2 tablespoons peanut butter mixture evenly over 1 side of tortilla, leaving a ½-inch border. Spread 1 tablespoon pineapple preserves over peanut butter mixture. Top with one-fourth of chicken, ⅓ cup shredded lettuce, and 2 teaspoons green onions. Roll up tortilla tightly. Do the same thing all over again with remaining peanut butter mixture, tortillas, pineapple preserves, chicken, lettuce, and green onions. Makes 4 wraps

FOR 1 WRAP: CALORIES 355 (39% from fat); FAT 15.4g (sat 2g, mono 1.3g, poly 1.3g); PROTEIN 27.9g; CARB 29.6g; FIBER 4.3g; CHOL 49mg; IRON 1.8mg; SODIUM 828mg; CALC 75mg

* see glossary

Tip: It's easier to serve these sandwiches when they're wrapped. Place each one onto a square of parchment or wax paper. Roll them up tightly, and twist the ends to seal. Cut the wraps in half, and peel back the paper as you eat.

**Prep: 30 min.
Cook: 15 min.**

TUNA FISH IN-a-FISH

UP TO THE CHALLENGE?

JUST FOR FUN

A hot and cheesy tuna salad wrapped in a fun pastry crust is sure to make a splash for supper.

1 (7.06-ounce) **package albacore tuna in water,** drained (we used Starkist)

1 cup (4 ounces) shredded **sharp Cheddar cheese**

¼ cup chopped **celery**

2 tablespoons **sweet or dill pickle relish**

1 tablespoon **Dijon mustard**

¼ teaspoon **pepper**

¼ cup **mayonnaise**

1 (15-ounce) **package refrigerated piecrust**

1 **large egg**

1 tablespoon **water**

Vegetable cooking spray

Decorations:
    Ranch dressing, celery slices, fish-shaped crackers

1 • *Preheat** oven to 425°.

2 • Combine first 6 ingredients in a big bowl. Add mayonnaise to tuna mixture, stirring gently until combined. Cover and *chill** in refrigerator.

3 • Unroll piecrusts. Stack piecrusts on a lightly floured surface, making sure they don't stick together. Divide dough into 4 equal portions using a pastry wheel, pizza wheel, or small knife. **a** Cut out 1 fish body from each portion of dough. **B** The bodies will resemble the shape of a football. Set fish body cut-outs aside, reserving scraps of dough.

• *Whisk** egg and 1 tablespoon water in a small bowl. Separate pastry into 8 fish cut-outs. Spoon one-fourth of tuna mixture in center of 1 fish cut-out, leaving a ½-inch border. Brush border with egg mixture.

• Place another fish cut-out on top of filling, pressing edges gently to seal. **C** Place stuffed piecrust on an ungreased baking sheet, and brush with egg mixture. Create eyes, tails, and fins from dough scraps, and attach to fish cut-out using the egg mixture like "glue." **D** Do the same thing all over again with remaining dough, tuna mixture, and egg mixture. Coat each fish with cooking spray.

4 • *Bake** at 425° for 15 minutes or until tails and edges of fish are golden brown. Remove baking sheet from the oven using oven mitts. Decorate serving plates with Ranch dressing, celery slices, and fish-shaped crackers, if you'd like. Makes 4 servings

FOR 1 SERVING: CALORIES 636 (59% from fat); FAT 41.4g (sat 15.1g, mono 0.2g, poly 0.2g); PROTEIN 20.7g; CARB 41.2g; FIBER 0.2g; CHOL 67mg; IRON 0.9mg; SODIUM 866mg; CALC 211mg

* see glossary

fish body

 MAIN COURSES

MEATBALL QUESADILLAS

Our kid testers recommend the quickest way to assemble the quesadillas: Set out all the ingredients on the counter in front of you, then put the quesadillas together like you are working on an assembly line.

½ (16-ounce) **jar spicy black bean dip** (we used Guiltless Gourmet)

12 (8-inch) **flour tortillas**

30 **frozen cooked meatballs,** thawed and coarsely chopped

1½ cups (6 ounces) shredded **Monterey Jack cheese**

1 **small green bell pepper,** diced

Toppings: sour cream, salsa

1 Assemble the quesadillas:
- *Spread** about 2 tablespoons bean dip evenly over 1 side of 6 tortillas. Top evenly with chopped meatballs, cheese, and bell pepper. Top with remaining tortillas.

2 • Cook quesadillas on a lightly *greased** griddle over medium heat 2 minutes on each side or until golden. Cut each quesadilla into wedges. Serve with toppings. Makes 6 servings

FOR 1 SERVING: CALORIES 693 (49% from fat); FAT 37.9g (sat 17.4g, mono 2.5g, poly 0.3g); PROTEIN 37.9g; CARB 47.4g; FIBER 8.8g; CHOL 75mg; IRON 3.1mg; SODIUM 1,177mg; CALC 337mg

Tip: If you don't have a griddle, use a lightly greased nonstick skillet to cook these quesadillas one at a time.

JUMPiN' JaCK JaMBaLaYa

"I used chicken instead of ham and turkey sausage when I made this recipe. It's healthier and still tasted great!" —Charlestan, Age 10

1⅔ cups uncooked **long-grain rice**

2 tablespoons **olive oil**

1 **large onion**, chopped

1 **red or green bell pepper**, chopped

8 **green onions**, chopped

2 **celery** ribs, chopped

3 cups **cubed ham**

1 pound **smoked sausage**, sliced

1 (14-ounce) **can chicken broth**

1 (8-ounce) **can tomato sauce**

1 teaspoon **Creole seasoning** (we used Tony Chachere)

1
- Cook rice according to package directions, omitting salt.
- While rice cooks, heat oil in a big skillet over medium heat. Add onion and next 3 ingredients; *sauté** until *tender**. *Stir** in ham, sausage, *broth**, tomato sauce, and Creole seasoning. Bring mixture to a *boil**; reduce heat, and *simmer** 20 minutes. Stir in hot cooked rice. Makes 8 servings

FOR 1 SERVING: CALORIES 449 (43% from fat); FAT 21.3g (sat 6.2g, mono 10.3g, poly 2.8g); PROTEIN 23.2g; CARB 40.1g; FIBER 1.9g; CHOL 72mg; IRON 3.5mg; SODIUM 1,504mg; CALC 35mg

* see glossary

Did you know

If foods could be related to one another like families, jambalaya would be a second cousin to gumbo, because the recipes are similar in flavor. The biggest difference is that the rice is mixed into jambalaya, and gumbo is served over rice.

CHUCK WAGON BARBECUE BEANS

Some kids like these meaty beans real thick. If you do too, cook them longer than 15 minutes but be sure to stir them often toward the end so they won't stick.

½ pound **ground pork sausage**

1 **medium onion,** chopped

½ **medium-size green bell pepper,** chopped

1 (15-ounce) **can pork and beans,** undrained

1 (16-ounce) **can pinto beans,** undrained

½ cup **ketchup**

⅓ cup firmly packed **light brown sugar**

1 teaspoon **dry mustard**

1 teaspoon **Worcestershire sauce**

1
- Cook sausage, onion, and pepper in a big skillet over medium-high heat, stirring until sausage crumbles and is no longer pink. *Drain** well, and return to skillet.
- *Stir** in beans and remaining ingredients. Cook over medium heat, stirring occasionally, 15 minutes or until thickened. Makes 4 servings

FOR 1 SERVING: CALORIES 455 (26% from fat); FAT 13.3g (sat 4.5g, mono 5.8g, poly 1.9g); PROTEIN 18.3g; CARB 67.1g; FIBER 11.9g; CHOL 38mg; IRON 4.6mg; SODIUM 1,407mg; CALC 127mg

* see glossary

**Prep: 20 min.
Cook: 25 min.**

CRISPY FISH STICKS

These oven-baked fish sticks are healthier than fried and just as crisp and delicious.

4 (1-ounce) slices **French bread,** torn into pieces

6 tablespoons **reduced-fat mayonnaise**

1 tablespoon **water**

1 teaspoon grated **lemon** rind

1½ teaspoons fresh **lemon** juice

1½ pounds **grouper or other firm white fish fillets**

Vegetable cooking spray

Quick-and-Easy Tartar Sauce (optional)

Ketchup (optional)

1 • *Preheat** oven to 425°.

2 • Place bread in the container of a food processor; top with cover. Process 30 seconds or until breadcrumbs are fine. Turn breadcrumbs out into a shallow dish.
 • *Stir** together mayonnaise and next 3 ingredients in a shallow bowl.
 • Cut fish into 1-inch-thick strips.

3 • Dip fish in mayonnaise mixture, and roll in breadcrumbs. Place fish on a big baking sheet coated with cooking spray.

4 • *Bake** at 425° for 25 minutes or until fish is golden and flakes with a fork. Remove baking sheet from the oven using oven mitts. Serve with Quick-and-Easy Tartar Sauce or ketchup, if you'd like. Makes 4 servings

FOR 1 SERVING: CALORIES 272 (19% from fat); FAT 5.6g (sat 1.3g, mono 0.7g, poly 0.7g); PROTEIN 35.5g; CARB 18g; FIBER 0.9g; CHOL 63mg; IRON 2.2mg; SODIUM 458mg; CALC 68mg

QUICK-AND-EASY TARTAR SAUCE

1 cup **reduced-fat mayonnaise**

¼ cup **sweet or dill pickle relish**

½ teaspoon grated **lemon** rind (optional)

2 tablespoons fresh **lemon** juice

1 • Stir together all ingredients in a small bowl until blended. Cover and *chill** in refrigerator up to 1 week. Makes 1¼ cups sauce

FOR 1 TABLESPOON: CALORIES 23 (63% from fat); FAT 1.6g (sat 0.4g, mono 0g, poly 0g); PROTEIN 0g; CARB 2.3g; FIBER 0g; CHOL 0mg; IRON 0mg; SODIUM 121mg; CALC 0mg

* see glossary

Alphabet
Chicken Soup,
page 108

SOUPS

Prep: 30 min.
Cook: 11 min.

CHUNKY CHEDDAR CHEESE CHOWDER

This chunky chowder will fill you up and keep you warm from head to toe.

¼ cup **butter or margarine**

1 **small onion,** chopped

2 **carrots,** chopped

1 **celery** rib, chopped

½ **small red or green bell pepper,** chopped

2 **garlic cloves,** minced

⅓ cup **all-purpose flour**

1 (14½-ounce) **can chicken broth**

2 cups **milk**

4 cups (16 ounces) shredded **Cheddar cheese**

½ teaspoon **salt**

¾ teaspoon **pepper**

4 **bacon slices,** cooked and crumbled

1 • *Melt** butter in a 3-quart saucepan over medium-high heat; *stir** in onion, carrot, celery, bell pepper, and garlic. *Sauté** 5 minutes or until mixture is *tender** and smells good.

• Add flour; cook 1 minute, stirring constantly. Stir in chicken *broth** and milk; cook over medium heat 5 minutes or until mixture is slightly thickened and bubbly.

2 • Add shredded cheese, salt, and pepper, stirring until cheese melts and mixture is smooth. Sprinkle with crumbled bacon. Makes 7 cups chowder

FOR 1 CUP: CALORIES 426 (68% from fat); FAT 32.3g (sat 19.6g, mono 9g, poly 1.2g); PROTEIN 21.3g; CARB 12.6g; FIBER 1g; CHOL 98mg; IRON 1mg; SODIUM 1,121mg; CALC 561mg

* see glossary

SPEEDY TEXAS CHILI

Thanks to a convenient boost from canned chili beans and bottled minced garlic, this hearty chili might just be the quickest in town.

1 pound **ground chuck**

1 **small onion**, chopped

1 teaspoon **bottled minced garlic**

1 (15.5-ounce) **can chili beans**, undrained (we used Bush's Best Chili Beans)

1 (6-ounce) **can tomato paste**

1½ cups **water**

1 tablespoon **chili powder**

1 teaspoon **salt**

Shredded **Cheddar cheese** (optional)

1 • Cook first 3 ingredients in a Dutch oven over medium-high heat, stirring until meat crumbles and is no longer pink. *Drain** well, and return to Dutch oven.

2 • *Stir** in beans and next 4 ingredients. Bring to a *boil**; reduce heat, and *simmer**, stirring occasionally, 15 minutes. Top each serving with Cheddar cheese, if you'd like. Makes 6 cups chili

FOR 1 CUP: CALORIES 255 (38% from fat); FAT 10.8g (sat 4.1g, mono 4.5g, poly 0.3g); PROTEIN 19g; CARB 18.8g; FIBER 5.3g; CHOL 52mg; IRON 2.6mg; SODIUM 762mg; CALC 28mg

* see glossary

QUICK CHICKEN AND DUMPLINGS

"My mom said this was the fastest chicken and dumpling recipe she's ever seen. We loved it and will probably have it again this week. My favorite part is cutting up the biscuits with kitchen shears." —Seth, Age 9

4 cups **water**

3 cups chopped **cooked chicken**

2 (10¾-ounce) **cans cream of chicken soup,** undiluted

2 teaspoons **chicken bouillon granules**

1 teaspoon **seasoned pepper**

1 (7.5-ounce) **can refrigerated buttermilk biscuits** (we used Pillsbury)

1 • Combine first 5 ingredients in a Dutch oven. Bring to a *boil** over medium-high heat, stirring often.

2 • Separate biscuits in half, forming 2 rounds; cut each round in half using kitchen shears.

• Drop biscuit pieces, 1 at a time, into boiling mixture; *stir** gently after each addition.

• Cover, reduce heat, and *simmer**, stirring occasionally, 15 to 20 minutes. Makes 8 cups chicken and dumplings

FOR 1 CUP: CALORIES 240 (33% from fat); FAT 8.8g (sat 2.4g, mono 1.6g, poly 1g); PROTEIN 19.3g; CARB 20.3g; FIBER 0.6g; CHOL 53mg; IRON 1.3mg; SODIUM 1,065mg; CALC 8mg

* see glossary

Tip: Use reduced-sodium, reduced-fat cream of chicken soup; reduced-fat biscuits; and chopped, cooked chicken breasts to reduce fat, sodium, and calories.

THICK 'N' CHUNKY POTATO SOUP

This recipe needs a big saucepan that has a tight-fitting lid.

1½ pounds **potatoes,** peeled and diced

1 **medium onion,** chopped

¼ cup chopped **celery**

1 (14-ounce) **can chicken broth**

1 teaspoon **chicken bouillon granules**

¼ teaspoon **salt**

⅛ teaspoon **pepper**

1½ cups **milk**

1 tablespoon **butter or margarine**

1 • Combine first 7 ingredients in a big saucepan. Bring to a *boil** over medium-high heat. Cover, reduce heat, and *simmer** 12 minutes or until potatoes are *tender** when you pierce them with a fork. *Stir** in milk and butter.

2 • Place half of soup mixture in a blender container; top with cover, and process until smooth. Return to saucepan; cook until thoroughly heated, stirring occasionally. Makes 5 cups soup

FOR 1 CUP: CALORIES 197 (25% from fat); FAT 5.5g (sat 2.9g, mono 1.2g, poly 0.3g); PROTEIN 6.2g; CARB 31.1g; FIBER 2.6g; CHOL 17mg; IRON 1.1mg; SODIUM 888mg; CALC 101mg

* see glossary

Prep: 1 min.
Cook: 4 min.

SUPERFAST & EASY

SOUPER-DUPER TOMATO SOUP

With so few ingredients and so little to do, you'll have this soup ready quickly, leaving you with plenty of time to play.

- 1 (14½-ounce) **can petite diced tomatoes,** undrained (we used Hunt's)
- 1 (10½-ounce) **can condensed tomato soup,** undiluted (we used Campbell's)
- ½ cup **half-and-half**
- **Pepper** (optional)

1 • Combine first 3 ingredients in a saucepan; cook over low heat until hot, stirring often. *Stir** in pepper, if you'd like. Makes 3 cups soup

FOR 1 CUP: CALORIES 152 (27% from fat); FAT 4.6g (sat 2.9g, mono 1.3g, poly 0.2g); PROTEIN 3.9g; CARB 24.5g; FIBER 3g; CHOL 15mg; IRON 1mg; SODIUM 768mg; CALC 64mg

* see glossary

Crouton Cut-Outs: Make toast just as you would for breakfast, and butter it if you'd like. Cut toast with cookie cutters, and serve with hot soup.

aLPHaBeT CHiCKeN SOUP

"I like to scoop up the letters and try to make words before I eat them. My name is hard to do because it's long, but my brother's name is Mac. It's easy!" —Natalie, Age 9

1 tablespoon **vegetable oil**

1 **medium onion,** chopped

2 **carrots,** chopped

2 **celery** ribs, chopped

2 **garlic cloves,** minced

2 (32-ounce) **containers reduced-sodium, fat-free chicken broth** (we used Swanson)

2 cups chopped **cooked chicken**

¼ teaspoon **dried thyme**

½ cup uncooked **alphabet-shaped pasta**

1 • Heat oil in a Dutch oven over medium-high heat until hot. *Stir** in onion, carrot, and celery. *Sauté** vegetables in hot oil 5 minutes; add garlic, and sauté 1 minute or until vegetables are *tender** and mixture smells good.

• Stir in *broth**, chicken, and thyme. Bring to a *boil**; reduce heat, and *simmer**, stirring occasionally, 15 minutes.

• Stir in pasta, and cook 8 minutes or just until pasta is tender. Makes 10 cups soup

FOR 1 CUP: CALORIES 111 (28% from fat); FAT 3.5g (sat 0.7g, mono 1.3g, poly 1.1g); PROTEIN 12g; CARB 7.9g; FIBER 0.8g; CHOL 25mg; IRON 0.6mg; SODIUM 562mg; CALC 16mg

* see glossary

Did you know?

Plants get thirsty just like people do. Try this experiment, and you'll see how plants drink. Start off with a few celery ribs with leaves. Give the ends opposite the leaves a fresh trim. Place the cut ends in a small container filled with water mixed with a little food coloring. Leave the celery there without disturbing it for about five hours.

At that time, you'll see that the celery sipped up the colored water through small veins called xylem (zi-lem). Celery and other plants sip water and nutrients from the soil in the very same way.

Corn On The Cob,
page 116

ON THE SIDE

MEXICAN RICE

This simple cumin-flavored rice looks and tastes like the authentic side dish from a Mexican restaurant.

1 cup uncooked **converted rice** (we used Uncle Ben's original converted rice)

1 **small onion**, finely chopped

1 tablespoon **vegetable oil**

½ teaspoon **ground cumin**

1 **garlic clove**, minced

1 (14-ounce) **can chicken broth**

⅓ cup **vegetable juice** (we used V8 vegetable juice)

2 teaspoons **tomato paste**

1
- Combine rice, onion, and oil in a medium saucepan. *Sauté** over medium heat, stirring constantly, 5 minutes or until mixture smells good and rice begins to brown.
- *Stir** in cumin and garlic. Sauté 30 seconds more, stirring constantly.

2
- Stir in chicken *broth**, vegetable juice, and tomato paste. Bring to a *boil** over medium-high heat.
- Cover, reduce heat, and *simmer** 20 minutes or until liquid is absorbed and rice is *tender**.
- Remove from heat, and let stand, covered, 5 minutes. Makes 6 servings

FOR 1 SERVING: CALORIES 155 (17% from fat); FAT 2.9g (sat 0.3g, mono 1g, poly 1g); PROTEIN 3.6g; CARB 28.2g; FIBER 0.5g; CHOL 3mg; IRON 1.1mg; SODIUM 464mg; CALC 18mg

* see glossary

GINGERED BABY CARROTS

These carrots would taste great with grilled pork chops for supper.

1 (16-ounce) **package baby carrots**, peeled

2 tablespoons **butter or margarine**

3 tablespoons **brown sugar**

3 tablespoons **orange juice**

½ teaspoon **ground ginger**

1 • Place carrots in a small saucepan. Add just enough water to cover carrots. Bring to a *boil**. Reduce heat, and cook 5 minutes or until carrots are *crisp-tender**.
 • *Drain** well.

2 • *Melt** butter in the same saucepan over medium-low heat. Add brown sugar, orange juice, and ginger, stirring until sugar *dissolves**. Add carrots, and *toss** gently to coat. Makes 4 servings

FOR 1 SERVING: CALORIES 121 (44% from fat); FAT 5.9g (sat 3.6g, mono 1.5g, poly 0.3g); PROTEIN 0.9g; CARB 17.3g; FIBER 2.1g; CHOL 15mg; IRON 1.2mg; SODIUM 132mg; CALC 45mg

* see glossary

**Prep: 6 min.
Cook: 22 min.**

CARROT FRIES*

GOOD FOR YOU

The vibrant orange color is a sign that these fries are a healthy choice.

1 (16-ounce) **package whole carrots**, peeled

1 tablespoon **olive oil**

½ teaspoon **salt**

¼ teaspoon **pepper**

Vegetable cooking spray

1 • *Preheat** oven to 475°.

2 • Cut away skinny tip and stem end of each carrot. Cut each carrot in half crosswise.
• Separate carrots into slender pieces and fat pieces. Cut slender pieces in half lengthwise. Cut fat pieces in half lengthwise, and then cut each half in half lengthwise again.
• Place carrots in a medium bowl, and *drizzle** with oil. *Toss** until carrots are coated with oil. Sprinkle with salt and pepper.

3 • Spray a jelly-roll pan with cooking spray. Place carrots on pan, and spread them out so they don't touch one another.
• *Bake** at 475° for 17 minutes. Turn carrots with a spatula, and bake 5 more minutes or until *tender** and browned. Makes 4 servings

FOR 1 SERVING: CALORIES 72 (45% from fat); FAT 3.6g (sat 0.5g, mono 2.5g, poly 0.5g); PROTEIN 1g; CARB 9.8g; FIBER 2.9g; CHOL 0mg; IRON 0.4mg; SODIUM 360mg; CALC 34mg

* see glossary

Cook: 7 min.

CORN ON THE COB

This might just be the easiest recipe in the world! You don't even need to remove the husks or silk from the corn before you begin.

4 ears **fresh corn with husks**

4 teaspoons **butter or margarine** (optional)

1 • Place corn 1 inch apart in the microwave. Microwave at HIGH 7 minutes, turning corn after 3½ minutes.

2 • Cool corn until it's not too hot to touch. Peel back husks, and remove silk. Serve with butter, if you'd like. Makes 4 servings

FOR 1 SERVING: CALORIES 77 (13% from fat); FAT 1.1g (sat 0.2g, mono 0.3g, poly 0.5g); PROTEIN 2.9g; CARB 17.1g; FIBER 2.4g; CHOL 0mg; IRON 0.5mg; SODIUM 14mg; CALC 2mg

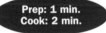

**Prep: 1 min.
Cook: 2 min.**

MICROWAVE BROCCOLI

After microwaving, remove the lid so the hot steam escapes away from your face.

1 (12-ounce) **package broccoli florets** (5 cups)

1 tablespoon **water**

2 tablespoons **butter or margarine** (optional)

¼ teaspoon **salt**

¼ teaspoon **pepper**

1 • Place broccoli and water in a 1½-quart baking dish that has a lid. Cover with lid. Microwave at HIGH 2 minutes or until *tender**. *Drain**. *Toss** with butter, if you'd like. Sprinkle with salt and pepper. Makes 4 servings

FOR 1 SERVING: CALORIES 25 (11% from fat); FAT 0.3g (sat 0.1g, mono 0g, poly 0.2g); PROTEIN 2.7g; CARB 4.7g; FIBER 2.6g; CHOL 0mg; IRON 0.8mg; SODIUM 169mg; CALC 43mg

* see glossary

GREEN BEANS

**Prep: 10 min.
Cook: 8 min.**

If you like green beans all by themselves, that's awesome! But if you'd like them spiffed up a little, try sprinkling them with Parmesan cheese or crumbled bacon. If you're more into dips, cool the beans to room temperature and serve them with Ranch dressing or salsa. Love salads? Some kids chill them until they're cold, and then drizzle them with a little Italian salad dressing.

2 pounds **fresh green beans,** trimmed

1 teaspoon **salt**

1 • Combine green beans and salt in a Dutch oven. Add just enough water to cover beans. Bring to a *boil**; cook over medium-high heat 6 minutes or until beans are desired degree of doneness. *Drain** well in a colander. Makes 8 servings

FOR 1 SERVING: CALORIES 35 (3% from fat); FAT 0.1g (sat 0g, mono 0g, poly 0.1g); PROTEIN 2.1g; CARB 8.1g; FIBER 3.9g; CHOL 0mg; IRON 1.2mg; SODIUM 104mg; CALC 42mg

* see glossary

Prep: 22 min.
Other: 30 min.

TROPICAL FRUIT SALAD

NO COOK

GOOD FOR YOU

This fruit salad is low in fat and calories. It could easily double as a healthy dessert.

3 **oranges,** peeled and sectioned

3 **kiwifruit,** peeled, quartered, and sliced

2 cups **fresh pineapple chunks**

2 **large bananas,** peeled and sliced

3 tablespoons **sweetened flaked coconut**

2 tablespoons **honey**

1 tablespoon fresh **lime** juice

1 tablespoon **orange juice**

1 cup **Creamy Brown Sugar Dressing**

1
- *Stir** together first 5 ingredients in a big bowl.
- *Whisk** together honey, lime juice, and orange juice in small bowl. *Drizzle** over fruit mixture. Cover with plastic wrap, and *chill** in refrigerator at least 30 minutes.

2
- Spoon ¾ cup fruit mixture into each of 8 small serving bowls; top each serving with 2 tablespoons Creamy Brown Sugar Dressing. Makes 8 servings

FOR 1 SERVING: CALORIES 178 (26% from fat); FAT 5.2g (sat 3.2g, mono 1.2g, poly 0.3g); PROTEIN 2.9g; CARB 33.1g; FIBER 3.7g; CHOL 13mg; IRON 0.6mg; SODIUM 50mg; CALC 76mg

Tip: Sectioning an orange might seem difficult at first. The more you do it, though, the easier it gets. Here's how: Using a paring knife, carefully slice away the peel and white pith from the orange. Hold the orange over a bowl to catch the juice. Carefully slice in between the sections as close to the edge as you can. Lift the segment out with the knife, and let it fall into the bowl.

CREAMY BROWN SUGAR DRESSING

1 (8-ounce) **package cream cheese,** softened

2 tablespoons **light brown sugar**

1 tablespoon **honey**

2 (6-ounce) **cartons low-fat vanilla yogurt**

½ teaspoon **ground cinnamon**

¼ teaspoon **coconut extract** (optional)

1
- *Beat** first 3 ingredients at medium speed with an electric mixer until creamy. Stir in yogurt, cinnamon, and coconut extract, if you'd like. Cover and chill in refrigerator up to 2 days. Makes 2½ cups

FOR 2 TABLESPOONS: CALORIES 61 (61% from fat); FAT 4.2g (sat 2.6g, mono 1.1g, poly 0.1g); PROTEIN 1.6g; CARB 4.6g; FIBER 0g; CHOL 13mg; IRON 0.2mg; SODIUM 44mg; CALC 36mg

* see glossary

Note: Serve leftovers of Creamy Brown Sugar Dressing as a dip for strawberries, grapes, or apple wedges.

**Prep: 12 min.
Cook: 1 hr., 1 min.**

STUFFED SWEET POTATOES

Melted marshmallows smother the buttery sweet potatoes and brown under the broiler in the oven. Ask a grown-up to help with that part of this recipe.

4 **small sweet potatoes** (about 8 ounces each)

2 tablespoons **vegetable oil**

¼ cup firmly packed **brown sugar**

2 tablespoons **butter or margarine**

1 teaspoon grated **orange rind**

⅓ cup fresh **orange** juice (about 1 orange)

¼ teaspoon **salt**

¼ teaspoon **ground nutmeg**

⅓ cup **chopped pecans** (optional)

1 cup **miniature marshmallows** (about 100)

1 • *Preheat** oven to 425°.

2 • Rub sweet potatoes with oil; place potatoes on a baking sheet. *Bake** at 425° for 1 hour or until potatoes are *tender**. Remove baking sheet from the oven using oven mitts, and let sweet potatoes cool until they feel warm but not too hot to touch.

3 • Preheat broiler.

4 • Cut skin off top of each potato. Using a small spoon, carefully scoop out pulp, leaving each shell in one piece. Combine potato pulp, brown sugar, and next 5 ingredients in a medium bowl; *beat** at low speed with an electric mixer until smooth. *Stir** in pecans, if you'd like.

5 • Spoon potato mixture evenly into shells. Press marshmallows in an even layer on top of filling in each sweet potato, completely covering the filling. Return potatoes to baking sheet.
• *Broil** 5 to 6 inches from heat 1 minute or until marshmallows are toasted and golden. Carefully remove baking sheet from the oven using oven mitts. Makes 4 servings

FOR 1 SERVING: CALORIES 303 (17% from fat); FAT 5.8g (sat 3.6g, mono 1.5g, poly 0.2g); PROTEIN 2.8g; CARB 60.1g; FIBER 5g; CHOL 15mg; IRON 1.3mg; SODIUM 299mg; CALC 66mg

* see glossary

Tip: To broil in step 5, move the oven rack so that the top of the marshmallows will be about 5 to 6 inches from the heat source.

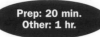

**Prep: 20 min.
Other: 1 hr.**

WALDORF SALAD

Next time you're in the supermarket, check out all the different colors and shapes of apples. Some are just right for baking because they hold their shape, and some are ideal for making applesauce because they don't! Apples that are great for snacking are great in salads, too. For this salad, try using Gala, Red Delicious, or Jonagold apples—they're nice and crisp served raw.

3 **large apples,** unpeeled, cored, and diced

1 cup **miniature marshmallows** (about 100) **or raisins**

½ cup chopped **celery**

½ cup chopped **walnuts or pecans**

½ cup **mayonnaise**

1
- Combine apples, marshmallows, celery, and walnuts in a medium bowl. Add mayonnaise, and *stir** to blend.
- Cover with plastic wrap, and *chill** in the refrigerator at least 1 hour. Makes 12 servings

FOR 1 SERVING: CALORIES 146 (68% from fat); FAT 11g (sat 1.3g, mono 2g, poly 1.1g); PROTEIN 0.6g; CARB 12g; FIBER 1.8g; CHOL 3mg; IRON 0.2mg; SODIUM 70mg; CALC 9mg

* see glossary

Did you know?

This simple salad got its name over 110 years ago from a fancy hotel in New York called The Waldorf=Astoria. Here's proof that anyone—not just a chef—can create a delicious recipe: Oscar Tschirky, the maître d'hôtel (or hotel's dining room manager) stirred together apples, celery, and mayonnaise in the original version. Chopped walnuts and other ingredients were added later. So take a tip from Oscar—get creative in the kitchen, and your recipe could be famous someday!

Flip-Floppin' Grape
Ice Cream, page 140

ROCKY TOP BROWNIES

JUST FOR FUN
LUNCHBOX FAVORITE

"Do I want to make these brownies again? Yes, yes, a million times yes, because they're real fun to make and they have peanut butter cups in them!" —Andrew, Age 5

1 (19.5-ounce) **package brownie mix** (we used Pillsbury traditional fudge)

½ cup **butter or margarine,** melted and cooled

3 **large eggs**

1 (13-ounce) **package miniature chocolate-covered peanut butter cups** (we used Reese's miniature peanut butter cups)

1 • *Preheat** oven to 350°.

2 • *Stir** together first 3 ingredients in a big bowl until blended. Spoon *batter** into a lightly *greased** 13- x 9-inch baking pan.
   • *Bake** at 350° for 23 minutes or just until center is *set**.

3 • While the brownies are baking, unwrap the peanut butter cups, and *chop** them.
   • Remove baking pan from the oven using oven mitts, and place on a wire rack. Top brownies with chopped peanut butter cups. Return pan to oven using oven mitts, and bake 2 more minutes.
   • Remove pan from the oven using oven mitts, and cool completely on a wire rack. Cut brownies into squares. Makes 2 dozen brownies

FOR 1 BROWNIE: CALORIES 227 (47% from fat); FAT 11.9g (sat 5g, mono 2.6g, poly 0.4g); PROTEIN 3.5g; CARB 26.8g; FIBER 0.4g; CHOL 38mg; IRON 0.8mg; SODIUM 148mg; CALC 4mg

* see glossary

MAKE-AHEAD

SUPERFAST & EASY

PEPPERMINT CANDY CRUNCH

Surprise your friends with a homemade gift from your kitchen.

30 **hard peppermint candies**

12 ounces **vanilla candy coating** (we used Candiquick Vanilla-flavored candy coating), broken into pieces

1 • Unwrap peppermint candies, and place in a zip-top freezer bag. Seal bag, removing as much air as you can. Wrap the bag in a kitchen towel, and crush candies using a rolling pin.

2 • Place candy coating in a big microwave-safe bowl; microwave at HIGH 1½ minutes or until coating looks like it's just beginning to *melt**. *Stir** candy coating until smooth. Stir in crushed peppermint.

3 • *Spread** mixture evenly onto a 15- x 10-inch jelly-roll pan lined with wax paper. *Chill** in the refrigerator 30 minutes or until candy is firm; break into pieces.

• Store in an airtight container up to 1 month. Makes 1 pound candy (16 ounces)

FOR 1 OUNCE: CALORIES 150 (34% from fat); FAT 5.7g (sat 4.3g, mono 0g, poly 0g); PROTEIN 0g; CARB 23.3g; FIBER 0g; CHOL 0mg; IRON 0mg; SODIUM 8mg; CALC 0mg

* see glossary

Prep: 12 min.
Other: 8 hrs., 25 min.

SUPERFAST & EASY

NO COOK

POLKA DOT ICE CREAM PIES

"Mixing up the lemonade and ice cream and plopping it into the tarts was easy. Next time, I'm using pink lemonade because pink is my favorite color!" —Anne Curtis, Age 7

1 quart **vanilla ice cream**

1 (6-ounce) **can frozen lemonade concentrate,** thawed and undiluted

12 (3-inch) **graham cracker tart shells**

Whipped topping (optional)

Round candy wafers (we used Necco Assorted Wafers) (optional)

1 • Let container of ice cream sit at *room temperature** 20 minutes to *soften**.
  • Spoon ice cream into a medium bowl. Add lemonade concentrate, and *whisk** until smooth. Pour into tart shells. Store tart shells in an airtight container in the freezer at least 8 hours or up to 2 weeks.

2 • Let tarts sit at room temperature 5 minutes before serving. Top with whipping topping and candy wafers, if you'd like. Makes 1 dozen tarts

FOR 1 TART: CALORIES 223 (42% from fat); FAT 10.4g (sat 4.1g, mono 3.9g, poly 1.7g); PROTEIN 2.5g; CARB 31.4g; FIBER 0.4g; CHOL 19mg; IRON 0.6mg; SODIUM 161mg; CALC 62mg

* see glossary

**Prep: 15 min.
Other: 8 hrs.**

COOKIES AND MILK PUDDING

MAKE-AHEAD

NO COOK

LUNCHBOX FAVORITE

"I had fun making this dessert for my family. It's special because everyone gets their own serving in these cute little bowls." —Callie, Age 8

3 **whole graham cracker sheets**

20 **chocolate chip cookies** (we used Nabisco Chunky Chips Ahoy)

¾ cup **milk**

1 (8-ounce) **container frozen whipped topping**, thawed

1 • Place graham crackers in a zip-top freezer bag. Seal bag, removing as much air as you can. Crush crackers using a rolling pin. ⓐ

2 • Sprinkle a heaping tablespoon of cracker crumbs in each of 6 (1-cup) containers with resealable lids. ⓑ

3 • Dip 1 cookie in milk for 10 seconds. ⓒ That's just enough time for the cookie to soften. Place the cookie on top of crumbs in 1 container. Do the same thing all over again with another cookie. *Spread** ¼ cup whipped topping over cookies. Dip 1 more cookie in milk, and place on top of whipped topping. Spread with ¼ cup whipped topping, sealing to edges.

4 • Do the same thing all over again with cookies, milk, and whipped topping. Crumble the last 2 cookies, and sprinkle over each serving. Seal containers with lids, and *chill** in the refrigerator at least 8 hours or up to 3 days. Makes 6 servings

FOR 1 SERVING: CALORIES 422 (51% from fat); FAT 23.9g (sat 9.3g, mono 0.5g, poly 0.3g); PROTEIN 4.5g; CARB 46.7g; FIBER 3.5g; CHOL 40mg; IRON 1.5mg; SODIUM 234mg; CALC 25mg

* see glossary

Prep: 4 min.
Cook: 6 min.
Other: 3 hrs.

SIMPLE VANILLA PUDDING

It's likely that you have all the ingredients for this recipe without going to the store.

¼ cup **sugar**

2 tablespoons **cornstarch**

⅛ teaspoon **salt**

2 cups **milk**

1 teaspoon **vanilla extract**

Whipped topping (optional)

Candy sprinkles (optional)

1 • Combine first 3 ingredients in a medium saucepan. *Whisk** in milk. Bring to a *boil** over medium heat, whisking constantly. Cook, stirring constantly, 1 minute or until pudding thickens. Remove from heat, and *stir** in vanilla.

2 • Pour pudding into a small bowl. Cool to *room temperature**, stirring occasionally. Cover with plastic wrap, and *chill** in the refrigerator at least 3 hours. Serve pudding with whipped topping and sprinkles, if you'd like. Makes 4 servings

FOR 1 SERVING: CALORIES 140 (26% from fat); FAT 4g (sat 2.3g, mono 1g, poly 0.2g); PROTEIN 3.9g; CARB 21.8g; FIBER 0g; CHOL 12mg; IRON 0.1mg; SODIUM 122mg; CALC 138mg

* see glossary

Did you know

American colonists used to make a jiggly dessert thickened with cornstarch called blancmange (blah-mahnzh).

By adding 2 more tablespoons cornstarch to this recipe, you can make blancmange. Stir in ¹/₄ teaspoon almond extract with the vanilla extract. Pour the superthick pudding into 6-ounce greased custard cups or fun molds. Cool and chill it just like the Simple Vanilla Pudding.

When you're ready to serve dessert, turn the molds upside down onto little plates, and let the desserts fall out. Top each with sweetened fresh berries or preserves, if you'd like.

Prep: 20 min.
Cook: 8 min. per batch
Other: 1 hr., 20 min.

ROLL 'N' CUT SUGAR COOKIES*

When you cut out cookies, press straight down into the dough—don't twist the cutter.

1 cup **butter**, softened

1 cup **sugar**

1 **large egg**

1 teaspoon **vanilla extract**

3 cups **all-purpose flour**

¼ teaspoon **salt**

Cream Frosting

Colored sugar or sugar sprinkles (optional)

1 Prepare the dough:
- Place butter in a big mixing bowl, and *beat** at medium speed with an electric mixer 2 minutes. Gradually add sugar, beating well. Add egg and vanilla, beating until blended.
- Combine flour and salt in a medium bowl; gradually add to butter mixture, beating just until blended. *Divide** dough in half; wrap each portion in plastic wrap, and *chill** in the refrigerator at least 1 hour.

2 • *Preheat** oven to 350°.

3 • *Roll** one portion of dough to ¼-inch thickness on a floured surface. Cut out cookies with 3-inch cookie cutters. Place 2 inches apart on lightly *greased** baking sheets.

4 • *Bake** at 350° for 8 minutes or until edges are lightly browned.
- Remove baking sheets from the oven using oven mitts. Cool cookies 2 minutes on baking sheets; remove to wire racks to cool completely.
- Do the same thing all over again with the other portion of dough.

5 • *Spread** cookies with Cream Frosting and sprinkle with colored sugar, if you'd like.
- Store cookies up to 1 week in an airtight container. Makes about 3½ dozen cookies

FOR 1 COOKIE: CALORIES 148 (36% from fat); FAT 5.9g (sat 3.6g, mono 1.6g, poly 0.3g); PROTEIN 1.2g; CARB 23.1g; FIBER 0.2g; CHOL 21mg; IRON 0.5mg; SODIUM 48mg; CALC 6mg

CREAM FROSTING

4 cups **powdered sugar**

½ cup plus 2 tablespoons **whipping cream**

½ teaspoon **lemon juice**

1 • *Stir** together all ingredients until smooth. Makes 2 cups frosting

FOR 1 TABLESPOON: CALORIES 74 (21% from fat); FAT 1.7g (sat 1.1g, mono 0.5g, poly 0.1g); PROTEIN 0.1g; CARB 15.1g; FIBER 0g; CHOL 6mg; IRON 0mg; SODIUM 2mg; CALC 3mg

* see glossary

Prep: 10 min.
Cook: 25 min.
Other: 30 min.

apple ENCHiLaDas

This dessert tastes like an apple pie but is way easier to make. You just roll up the apple mixture in flour tortillas!

1 (21-ounce) **can apple fruit filling**

6 (6-inch) **flour tortillas**

1 teaspoon **ground cinnamon**

½ cup **granulated sugar**

½ cup firmly packed **light brown sugar**

½ cup **water**

⅓ cup **butter or margarine**

Whipped cream (optional)

1 • Spoon fruit filling evenly down center of each tortilla, and sprinkle with cinnamon. Roll up each tortilla, and place, seam side down, in a lightly *greased** 2-quart baking dish. Set aside apple enchiladas.

2 • Combine granulated sugar and next 3 ingredients in a medium saucepan. Bring to a *boil** over medium heat; reduce heat, and *simmer**, stirring constantly, 3 minutes.
• Pour sauce over apple enchiladas; let stand 30 minutes.

3 • *Preheat** oven to 350°.

4 • *Bake** at 350° for 20 minutes. Remove from oven using oven mitts. Serve warm with whipped cream, if you'd like. Makes 6 servings

FOR 1 SERVING: CALORIES 424 (27% from fat); FAT 12.7g (sat 7g, mono 3.9g, poly 0.9g); PROTEIN 2.9g; CARB 77.3g; FIBER 2.2g; CHOL 27mg; IRON 1.9mg; SODIUM 326mg; CALC 69mg

* see glossary

**Prep: 25 min.
Cook: 12 min. per batch
Other: 2 min.**

CHOCOLATE CHIPPERS

"The fun part about making this recipe is cooking with Mommy and nibbling on the chocolate chips!" —Will, Age 4

½ cup **butter or margarine**, softened

½ cup **shortening**

¾ cup firmly packed **light brown sugar**

½ cup **granulated sugar**

1 **large egg**

1 teaspoon **vanilla extract**

2 cups **all-purpose flour**

1 teaspoon **baking soda**

½ teaspoon **salt**

2 cups (12 ounces) **semisweet chocolate morsels**

1 cup **chopped pecans** (optional)

1 • *Preheat** oven to 350°.

2 • Place butter and shortening in a big mixing bowl, and *beat** at medium speed with an electric mixer until creamy. Gradually add sugars, beating until blended. Add egg and vanilla, beating well.
• Combine flour, soda, and salt in a medium bowl; gradually add to butter mixture, beating until blended. *Stir** in chocolate morsels and pecans, if you'd like.

3 • Drop dough by rounded tablespoonfuls onto ungreased baking sheets. *Bake** at 350° for 12 minutes or until lightly browned.

4 • Remove baking sheets from the oven using oven mitts. Let cool 2 minutes on baking sheets. Remove cookies to wire racks to cool completely.
• Store cookies in an airtight container up to 1 week. Makes about 5 dozen cookies

FOR 1 COOKIE: CALORIES 102 (57% from fat); FAT 6.5g (sat 2.5g, mono 2.6g, poly 1.1g); PROTEIN 1g; CARB 11.4g; FIBER 0.6g; CHOL 8mg; IRON 0.5mg; SODIUM 54mg; CALC 7mg

* see glossary

Tip: Nothing beats a warm chocolate chip cookie. Refrigerate a batch of this dough in an airtight container up to 1 week and enjoy cookies fresh from the oven anytime.

FLIP-FLOPPIN' GRAPE ICE CREAM

NO COOK

JUST FOR FUN

No ice cream freezer needed here—two plastic freezer bags make an amazing substitute. It's important to be sure the bags are sealed completely to prevent leaking. So doublecheck them before the fun begins.

¾ cup **powdered sugar**

½ cup **half-and-half**

½ cup **grape juice**

⅓ cup **whipping cream**

1 teaspoon **lemon juice**

¾ cup **rock salt**

Crushed ice

1 • Combine first 5 ingredients in a medium bowl, stirring until sugar *dissolves**. Pour creamy grape mixture into a 1-quart zip-top freezer bag; carefully seal bag.

• Place about half of rock salt, about 2 cups crushed ice, and the sealed 1-quart bag in a 1-gallon zip-top freezer bag. Carefully seal 1-gallon bag.

2 • Place bag on a flat surface. Gently *flip** bag, end over end, for 5 minutes. Open the 1-gallon bag over a sink, and *drain** water. Add remaining rock salt and enough ice to fill bag again. Carefully reseal.

• Continue to gently flip bag, end over end, 15 more minutes. If your arms get tired, rest for about 1 minute.

3 • Open the 1-gallon bag over a sink again, and drain water. Throw away the 1-gallon bag filled with rock salt. Wipe the 1-quart bag filled with ice cream dry. *Snip** 1 corner with kitchen shears, and squeeze ice cream into individual bowls. Makes 1½ cups ice cream

FOR ½ CUP: CALORIES 278 (44% from fat); FAT 13.5g (sat 8.2g, mono 4g, poly 0.2g); PROTEIN 1.2g; CARB 38.7g; FIBER 0g; CHOL 50mg; IRON 0.1mg; SODIUM 26mg; CALC 60mg

* see glossary

Did you know?

Making ice cream is simply a matter of sharing. Heat energy, that is. Believe it or not, the creamy grape mixture in step 1 has heat energy, and to become ice cream it must totally get rid of it. Now for ice to melt it needs the heat energy—right? Of course! That's why in step 2 we put them very close together so the creamy grape mixture could share its heat energy with ice and transform into ice cream!

TRIPLE-CHOCOLATE CAKE

Make stencils of hearts, stars, circles, or triangles from small sheets of wax paper. Place the stencil on each square of cake, and sprinkle with powdered sugar. Carefully take off the stencil to show off the designs.

1 (18.25-ounce) **package devil's food cake mix**

1 (3.9-ounce) **package chocolate instant pudding mix**

2 cups **sour cream**

1 cup **butter or margarine,** softened

5 **large eggs**

1 teaspoon **vanilla extract**

2 cups **semisweet chocolate morsels**

Powdered sugar (optional)

1 • *Preheat** oven to 350°.

2 • Combine first 6 ingredients in a big mixing bowl, and *beat** at low speed with an electric mixer 30 seconds or just until moistened. Increase to medium speed, and beat 2 more minutes. *Stir** in chocolate morsels; pour *batter** evenly into 2 *greased** and floured 9-inch square cake pans.

3 • *Bake** at 350° for 25 to 30 minutes or until a wooden pick inserted in center comes out clean. Remove pans from the oven using oven mitts. Let cool completely in pans on wire racks. Cut into squares, and sprinkle with powdered sugar, if you'd like. Makes 18 servings

FOR 1 SERVING: CALORIES 495 (59% from fat); FAT 32.3g (sat 19.3g, mono 9.6g, poly 1.2g); PROTEIN 6.1g; CARB 50.2g; FIBER 2.6g; CHOL 97mg; IRON 2.1mg; SODIUM 366mg; CALC 71mg

* see glossary

ALMOST SNOW CREAM

Snow cream is a slushy wintertime treat made from freshly fallen snow. This recipe is a lot like it and can be made anytime of the year.

4 cups **milk**

⅓ cup **sugar**

⅛ teaspoon **salt**

2 teaspoons **vanilla extract**

1 • Combine all ingredients in the can of a 2-quart electric ice cream maker, stirring until sugar *dissolves**. Freeze according to manufacturer's directions. Serve slushy. Makes 1 quart ice cream

FOR ½ **CUP:** CALORIES 109 (33% from fat); FAT 4g (sat 2.3g, mono 1g, poly 0.2g); PROTEIN 3.9g; CARB 14g; FIBER 0g; CHOL 12mg; IRON 0mg; SODIUM 85mg; CALC 138mg

Hot Vanilla Milk:

• Combine all Almost Snow Cream ingredients in a 1-quart microwave-safe measuring cup, stirring gently until sugar dissolves. Microwave at HIGH 5 minutes or until hot, stirring once. Pour into mugs. Top with marshmallows, if you'd like. Makes 4 servings

FOR 1 SERVING: CALORIES 218 (33% from fat); FAT 8g (sat 4.6g, mono 2g, poly 0.4g); PROTEIN 7.8g; CARB 28g; FIBER 0g; CHOL 24mg; IRON 0mg; SODIUM 170mg; CALC 276mg

* see glossary

Fantastic Flans,
page 150

CRUNCHY MUNCHY LETTUCE WRAPS

In Asian cultures, lettuce wraps are often served for dim sum, a meal made from a sampling of several different kinds of foods. But lettuce wraps make a great meal all by themselves, too.

1 pound **ground turkey** (light and dark meat)

1 tablespoon **peanut or canola oil**

1 (8-ounce) **can bamboo shoots,** drained and minced

1 (8-ounce) **can sliced water chestnuts,** drained and minced

½ (8-ounce) **package sliced fresh mushrooms,** minced

4 **green onions,** minced

½ cup **frozen sweet peas**

½ cup **sesame ginger 30-minute marinade** (we used Lawry's)

12 **iceberg lettuce leaves**

Sesame ginger 30-minute marinade (optional)

1 • Cook turkey in a big nonstick skillet over medium-high heat, stirring until it crumbles and is no longer pink; *drain** well in a colander. Set aside.

2 • Add oil to pan, and place pan over medium-high heat until hot. Add bamboo shoots and next 3 ingredients. *Stir-fry** 1 to 2 minutes. *Stir** in peas, ½ cup marinade, and cooked turkey. Cook, stirring constantly, until thoroughly heated.

3 • Spoon about ½ cup turkey mixture onto each lettuce leaf; fold leaves in half. Dip lettuce wraps in marinade, if you'd like. Makes 6 servings

FOR 1 SERVING: CALORIES 394 (22% from fat); FAT 9.5g (sat 2.2g, mono 3.7g, poly 2.5g); PROTEIN 28.1g; CARB 51.3g; FIBER 13.6g; CHOL 55mg; IRON 5.8mg; SODIUM 976mg; CALC 265mg

* see glossary

Tip: It's easiest to eat lettuce wraps "soft taco-style" with big lettuce leaves. To cut a head of iceberg lettuce in half, begin at the core end, and then gently separate the lettuce into leaves, trying to keep them in big pieces.

FaNTasTic FLaNS

This silky Spanish custard is traditionally served with golden melted sugar dripping in a pool around it. Making melted sugar is an advanced cooking skill you'll learn when you're older. Our version, using melted caramels, is easier and tastes similar.

8 **caramels**, unwrapped
(we used Kraft)

2 **large eggs**

3 tablespoons **sugar**

1⅓ cups **whole milk**

⅛ teaspoon **salt**

½ teaspoon **vanilla extract**

1 • *Preheat** oven to 325°.

2 • Place 2 caramels in each of 4 (6-ounce) custard cups. Microwave at HIGH 20 seconds or until caramels look like they're beginning to *melt**. *Stir** caramels so melted candy will be flat in the bottom of each custard cup. Set custard cups in a 9-inch square pan.

3 • *Whisk** together eggs and remaining ingredients in a medium bowl until blended. Carefully pour mixture evenly into prepared cups. Add hot water to pan until it's 1 inch deep (see tip below).
• *Bake** at 325° for 45 minutes or until a knife inserted just off center in each custard cup comes out clean.
• Carefully remove pan from the oven using oven mitts. Carefully remove flans from hot water, and cool completely on a wire rack. Cover and *chill** in refrigerator overnight or up to 3 days.

4 • Run a small knife around edge of 1 flan to loosen. *Invert** flan onto a small dessert plate. Scrape any extra caramel onto flan. Do the same thing all over again with remaining flans. Makes 4 servings

FOR 1 SERVING: CALORIES 191 (30% from fat); FAT 6.3g (sat 2.7g, mono 1.6g, poly 0.5g); PROTEIN 6.6g; CARB 26.1g; FIBER 0g; CHOL 116mg; IRON 0.5mg; SODIUM 184mg; CALC 137mg

* see glossary

Tip: Use a liquid measuring cup with a spout or a small pitcher to fill the baking pan with hot water in step 3. It will help you pour more accurately so you won't get water in any of the custard cups.

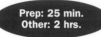

**Prep: 25 min.
Other: 2 hrs.**

REDCOAT TRIFLE

MAKE-AHEAD

NO COOK

Here's a delicious math problem: sweetened strawberries + pound cake + vanilla pudding + whipped cream = a British dessert called trifle.

1 (10-ounce) **package frozen unsweetened strawberries,** thawed

1½ cups **strawberry jam,** divided

1 (10.75-ounce) **frozen pound cake,** thawed and cut into ¼-inch slices

1 (3.4-ounce) **package vanilla instant pudding mix**

1½ cups **milk**

1½ cups **frozen whipped topping,** thawed

2 tablespoons **orange juice**

2 cups sliced **fresh strawberries**

Strawberry slices (optional)

1 • Combine thawed strawberries and 1 cup jam in a food processor or blender; top with cover, and process until smooth. **ⓐ** Set aside.

2 • *Spread** remaining jam in between cake slices like you're making strawberry jam sandwiches. Cut sandwiches into 1-inch cubes. **Ⓑ** Set aside.

3 • Prepare pudding mix according to package directions, using 1½ cups milk. Gently *fold** in 1½ cups whipped topping. **Ⓒ**

4 • Spoon one-third of strawberry mixture into a 2-quart trifle bowl; top with half of cake cubes. *Drizzle** with 1 tablespoon orange juice. Spread half of pudding mixture over cake cubes, and top with 1 cup sliced fresh strawberries. **Ⓓ**

• Do the same thing all over again with strawberry mixture, cake cubes, orange juice, pudding mixture, and sliced fresh strawberries. Drizzle remaining strawberry mixture over the top.

• Cover with plastic wrap, and *chill** in the refrigerator at least 2 hours or up to 2 days. Top with more strawberry slices before serving, if you'd like. Makes 12 servings

FOR 1 SERVING: CALORIES 549 (46% from fat); FAT 28.3g (sat 15.9g, mono 0.3g, poly 0.1g); PROTEIN 7.9g; CARB 93.6g; FIBER 2.6g; CHOL 186mg; IRON 3.2mg; SODIUM 288mg; CALC 85mg

* see glossary

Note: A glass trifle bowl makes it easy to admire the pretty layers, but any 2-quart bowl will do.

Prep: 10 min.
Cook: 20 min.

BAKED GNOCCHI WITH CHEESE

Gnocchi (NYOK-kee) is an Italian specialty. It's a small dumpling made from potatoes, flour, and eggs. If you like pasta, you'll love gnocchi.

1 (32-ounce) **container chicken broth**

1 (16-ounce) **package vacuum-packed gnocchi**

4 **plum tomatoes,** coarsely chopped

1 tablespoon **butter or margarine**

¼ teaspoon **pepper**

1 cup (4 ounces) shredded **mozzarella cheese**

¼ cup grated **Parmesan cheese**

1 • *Preheat** broiler.

2 • Place *broth** in a Dutch oven. Add enough water to equal the amount you need to cook gnocchi according to the package directions. Prepare gnocchi as directed. *Drain** and return to Dutch oven.
• Add tomatoes, butter, and pepper. *Toss** gently until butter melts.

3 • Spoon mixture into 8 lightly *greased** (8-ounce) ovenproof ramekins or a lightly greased 11- x 8-inch baking dish. Sprinkle with cheeses.

4 • *Broil** 5 to 6 inches from heat 3 minutes or until cheese is bubbly and lightly browned. Remove dish from the oven using oven mitts. Makes 8 servings

FOR 1 SERVING: CALORIES 166 (31% from fat); FAT 5.7g (sat 3.1g, mono 0.6g, poly 0.1g); PROTEIN 7.4g; CARB 23.1g; FIBER 1.1g; CHOL 15mg; IRON 0.6mg; SODIUM 587mg; CALC 130mg

* see glossary

Did you know

A sharp knife is safer than a dull knife. That's because you don't have to push as hard. And if you don't have to push as hard, the knife probably won't slip and hurt you.

FLAKY CREAM CHEESE STRUDEL

UP TO THE CHALLENGE?

Strudel is a filled pastry that was created in Germany. Traditional strudel dough is very difficult to make, so our recipe uses phyllo dough, which you can buy already made.

1 (8-ounce) **package cream cheese,** softened

3 tablespoons **granulated sugar**

1 **egg** yolk

½ cup **golden raisins**

2 teaspoons grated **lemon** rind

4 sheets **phyllo pastry**

½ cup **butter,** melted and cooled

¼ cup **fine, dry breadcrumbs**

Sifted **powdered sugar** (optional)

1 • *Preheat** oven to 375°.

2 • *Beat** cream cheese at medium speed with an electric mixer until creamy. Add sugar, beating 1 to 2 minutes. Add egg yolk, and beat just until blended. *Stir** in raisins and lemon *rind**. Cover with plastic wrap, and *chill** in the refrigerator.

3 • Place 1 sheet of phyllo on a big piece of wax paper. Brush with melted butter using a pastry brush; sprinkle with 1 tablespoon breadcrumbs. Top with another sheet of phyllo, brush with melted butter, and sprinkle with 1 tablespoon breadcrumbs. Do the same thing all over again with remaining phyllo, melted butter, and breadcrumbs.
• Notice that the stack of phyllo is shaped like a rectangle. *Spread** cheese mixture down one short side of rectangle, leaving a 1-inch margin around the edges.
• Fold the long sides over the cream cheese mixture about 1 inch so it won't ooze out when it's rolled up. Roll it up, starting with the short side that has cream cheese on it.

4 • Carefully move roll to a big *greased** baking sheet. Turn it so that the seam is on the bottom. Brush strudel with remaining melted butter.
• *Bake** at 375° for 25 to 30 minutes or until golden. Remove baking sheet from the oven using oven mitts. Carefully slide strudel to a wire rack, and cool at least 30 minutes. Cut into 1-inch pieces, and sprinkle with powdered sugar, if you'd like. Makes 6 servings

FOR 1 SERVING (2 PIECES): CALORIES 391 (69% from fat); FAT 30.1g (sat 18.4g, mono 8.4g, poly 1.4g); PROTEIN 5.4g; CARB 27g; FIBER 1g; CHOL 116mg; IRON 1.4mg; SODIUM 316mg; CALC 55mg

* see glossary

Tip: You'll find phyllo pastry in supermarkets on the frozen food aisle. It's important to *thaw** it completely before you use it. Once you open the package, keep it covered with a damp towel as you work on the recipe; this will keep it from becoming dry and brittle.

PRONTO PASTITSIO

"My family goes to a Greek food festival every year, and I eat pastitsio because it's my favorite. Now I don't have to wait—I can make it anytime!" —Sophia, Age 9

6 ounces uncooked **elbow macaroni**

1 pound **ground lamb or ground chuck**

½ cup chopped **onion**

¼ teaspoon **salt**

2 cups **tomato-and-basil pasta sauce** (we used Prego)

¼ teaspoon **ground cinnamon**

1 (10-ounce) **container fresh Alfredo sauce** (we used Buitoni)

1½ cups (6 ounces) **shredded 6-cheese Italian blend** (we used Sargento)

1 • *Preheat** oven to 350°.

2 • Cook macaroni according to package directions; *drain** in a colander, and set aside.

3 • Meanwhile, cook ground lamb, onion, and salt in a big skillet over medium-high heat, stirring until meat crumbles and is no longer pink. Drain well in a colander, and return to skillet. *Stir** in pasta sauce and cinnamon. Bring to a *boil**; reduce heat, and *simmer**, uncovered, 5 minutes, stirring occasionally.

4 • Spoon half of macaroni into a lightly *greased** 11- x 7-inch baking dish; top with meat mixture. Spoon remaining macaroni over meat mixture. *Spread** Alfredo sauce over macaroni, and sprinkle with cheese.

5 • *Bake** at 350° for 30 minutes or until browned and bubbly. Remove dish from the oven using oven mitts. Let stand 5 minutes before serving. Makes 6 servings

FOR 1 SERVING: CALORIES 488 (49% from fat); FAT 26.7g (sat 13.7g, mono 4.3g, poly 0.9g); PROTEIN 28g; CARB 33.5g; FIBER 2.5g; CHOL 97mg; IRON 2.5mg; SODIUM 1,079mg; CALC 351mg

* see glossary

Tip: To make Pronto Pastitsio ahead, prepare the recipe through step 4. Cover it with plastic wrap, and *chill** in the refrigerator overnight. Uncover and bake the next day at 350° for 40 minutes or until browned and bubbly.

Did you know?

Pastitsio (pah-STEET-see-oh) is a Greek casserole made with layers of pasta, meat sauce, and a creamy white sauce. The traditional meat is lamb because more sheep are raised in Greece than cattle. It tastes great with beef, too.

Prep: 25 min.
Cook: 23 min., 40 sec.
Other: 30 min.

VIVA LES GALETTES

If you ask a Frenchman, "What is a galette?" you might get more than one answer. That's because a galette (gah-LEHT) can be sweet like a fruit pie or savory like a cheese pizza. Either way, they're all flat like a pancake. Our version is sweet with a flaky crust and a fruit filling.

Vegetable cooking spray

1 (8-ounce) **package cream cheese**, softened

1 (12-ounce) **can sweetened condensed milk**

1 (15-ounce) **package refrigerated piecrusts**

1 **egg** white, lightly beaten

1 tablespoon **sugar**

⅔ cup **peach fruit spread**

8 **strawberries**, stems removed and sliced

2 **kiwifruit**, peeled, sliced, and halved

1 cup **blueberries**

1 (11-ounce) **can mandarin oranges**, drained

1 • *Preheat** oven to 375°. Line 2 baking sheets with aluminum foil, and spray generously with cooking spray. Set aside.

2 • *Beat** cream cheese at medium speed with an electric mixer until creamy. Gradually add milk, beating until smooth. Set aside.

3 • Unroll piecrusts, and then *roll** into 13-inch circles on prepared baking sheets. *Spread** half of cream cheese mixture on top of each circle, leaving a 1½-inch border. Fold edges of dough toward center, pressing gently to seal. (Dough will cover only the outside edge.)
• Brush edges of galettes with egg white using a pastry brush, and sprinkle with sugar. *Bake** at 375° for 23 minutes or until filling is *set** and pastry is lightly browned. Remove baking sheets from the oven using oven mitts. Carefully slide galettes to a wire rack, and cool completely.

4 • Place fruit spread in a small microwave-safe bowl. Microwave at HIGH 30 to 40 seconds until melted. Brush over pastry using a pastry brush. Top with fruit. *Chill** in the refrigerator at least 30 minutes. Makes 12 servings

FOR 1 SERVING: CALORIES 382 (43% from fat); FAT 18.4g (sat 9g, mono 2.6g, poly 0.4g); PROTEIN 5.1g; CARB 49.7g; FIBER 1g; CHOL 34mg; IRON 0.5mg; SODIUM 243mg; CALC 105mg

* see glossary

Did you know?
Sweetened condensed milk is a sticky but yummy ingredient that's often used in desserts. Its name reveals exactly what it is—whole milk that's been condensed. That means the milk has been heated until most of the water evaporates, leaving it rich and concentrated. At the end, it's sweetened with sugar.

Prep: 35 min.
Cook: 10 min.
Other: 45 min.

SAINT LUCIA'S DAY BUNS

MAKE-AHEAD

UP TO THE CHALLENGE?

December 13—Saint Lucia's Day—is the beginning of the Scandinavian Christmas season. Many years ago it was tradition on that day for the eldest daughter in a family to serve her parents coffee and these pretty rolls. When she did, she'd wear a white gown and a candle-studded wreath on her head. Have you ever seen that image on a Christmas card?

1 (¼-ounce) **envelope active dry yeast**

½ cup warm **water** (100° to 110°)

¼ teaspoon **saffron threads**

2 teaspoons hot tap **water**

¼ cup **butter or margarine,** melted and cooled

1 **large egg**

2 tablespoons **sugar**

1 teaspoon **salt**

2¼ cups **all-purpose flour**

½ cup **golden raisins**

1 **large egg,** lightly beaten

1 Make the dough:
- *Stir** together *yeast** and ½ cup warm water in a medium mixing bowl; let stand 5 minutes.
- Meanwhile, combine saffron and 2 teaspoons hot tap water in a small bowl; let stand 5 minutes. *Drain** saffron mixture through a fine metal sieve directly into dissolved yeast. Throw away the saffron threads.
- *Whisk** butter, 1 egg, sugar, and salt into the yeast mixture until blended. Stir in 2 cups flour to make a soft dough.
- Turn dough out onto a lightly floured surface. *Knead** until smooth and stretchy, adding additional flour if dough is too sticky (about 5 minutes).

2 Shape the dough, and let it rise:
- *Divide** dough into 9 equal portions; shape each portion into a 12-inch rope. Working on lightly *greased** baking sheets, make an S-shape with each rope, making sure the ends are coiled tightly in opposite directions toward middle of rope.
- Cover and let *rise** in a warm place (85°), free from drafts, 35 minutes or until doubled in size.

3
- *Preheat** oven to 375°.

4
- Place a raisin in the center of each coiled end, and gently brush buns with beaten egg using a pastry brush. *Bake** at 375° for 10 minutes or until lightly browned. Carefully remove baking sheets from the oven using oven mitts. Makes 9 buns

FOR 1 BUN: CALORIES 212 (28% from fat); FAT 6.5g (sat 3.6g, mono 1.8g, poly 0.5g); PROTEIN 5.2g; CARB 33.4g; FIBER 1.3g; CHOL 60mg; IRON 1.9mg; SODIUM 312mg; CALC 17mg

* see glossary

Tip: If you can resist eating these special buns warm, cool them completely, and store in an airtight container in the freezer up to 1 month.

HaMANTASCHEN iN a HURRY

These delicious cookies are a traditional treat during Purim, the Jewish celebration of the deliverance from an evil scheme by Haman, advisor to the king of Persia. The cookies' shape resembles Haman's three-cornered hat.

Vegetable cooking spray

¼ cup **sugar**

1 (15-ounce) **package refrigerated piecrusts**

¾ cup **apricot preserves**

1 • *Preheat** oven to 375°. Line a big baking sheet with aluminum foil, and spray generously with cooking spray. Set aside.

2 • Place sugar in a shallow dish.

3 • Unroll piecrusts, and then *roll** them into 12-inch circles; cut each crust into 14 (2½-inch) circles, using a round cookie cutter. Throw away excess piecrust. Gently *dredge** both sides of each circle in sugar, and place on prepared baking sheet.
  • Place 1 rounded teaspoonful of apricot preserves in center of 1 circle. Brush edges of circle with water using a pastry brush. Lift edges to center over filling, forming a triangle. Pinch triangle points firmly to seal, and press edges of pastry toward center (see tip below).
  • Do the same thing all over again with the remaining apricot preserves and pastry circles.

4 • *Bake** at 375° for 11 minutes or until lightly browned. Remove baking sheet from the oven using oven mitts. Let cookies stand 5 minutes on baking sheet. Using a spatula, move to wire racks to cool completely. Makes 28 cookies

FOR 1 COOKIE: CALORIES 62 (29% from fat); FAT 2g (sat 0.7g, mono 0g, poly 0g); PROTEIN 0.1g; CARB 11g; FIBER 0g; CHOL 1mg; IRON 0mg; SODIUM 31mg; CALC 0mg

* see glossary

Tip: It's important that the triangle points are pinched firmly and that the pastry edges are pressed to lean toward the centers. This helps the cookies keep their triangular shape as they bake.

Beary Good Rolls,
page 173

FUN FOOD

INCREDIBLE EDIBLE NUTTY PUTTY

"I could measure and add everything for this recipe just fine. When I poured in the milk powder, it got real dusty. I stirred slow then fast. I wish I could make Nutty Putty every day because it's so fun!" —Andrew, Age 5

1 cup **creamy peanut butter**

3 tablespoons **honey**

1 cup **instant nonfat dry milk**

Decorations: colored sugar, candy sprinkles, raisins (optional)

1 • *Stir** together peanut butter and honey in a big bowl. Add dry milk, stirring until blended. Spoon a small amount onto a plate. Shape and decorate it anyway you wish before gobbling it up.

• Store remaining putty in the refrigerator in an airtight container up to 1 week. Makes 1½ cups

FOR 1 TABLESPOON: CALORIES 81 (59% from fat); FAT 5.3g (sat 1g, mono 0g, poly 0g); PROTEIN 3.7g; CARB 6g; FIBER 0.7g; CHOL 0mg; IRON 0.3mg; SODIUM 66mg; CALC 38mg

* see glossary

**Prep: 20 min.
Other: 1 hr.**

CARROT-ORANGE CARICATURES

GOOD FOR YOU

UP TO THE CHALLENGE?

JUST FOR FUN

Hollowed out oranges are perfect for holding single servings of this healthy carrot salad. Adding a silly face makes mealtime fun!

6 **navel oranges**

½ cup **light mayonnaise**

1 teaspoon **lemon juice**

4 cups shredded **carrot** (about 6 large)

½ cup **raisins**

Additional ingredients: shredded or grated carrot, sliced celery, halved grapes, kiwi slices, celery leaves, sweet red pepper pieces, dried apricots, raisins, blueberries, parsley, peanut butter, curly lettuce (optional)

1
- Cut a thin slice from stem end of each orange so it will sit flat. Cut a ¾-inch slice from top of each orange.
- Ask a grown-up to clip the membranes inside each orange shell using kitchen shears. Dig out pulp using a big spoon. Set aside. Squeeze pulp over a bowl to get juice out.
- Put ¼ cup orange juice in a big bowl. (Save the rest to drink later.) *Whisk** in mayonnaise and lemon juice. *Stir** in carrot and raisins. Cover and *chill** salad and orange shells in refrigerator at least 1 hour.

2
- Fill each orange shell with salad. With additional ingredients, make each serving into a face like this: Use shredded or grated carrot to resemble hair. Attach additional ingredients to orange shells to resemble faces using peanut butter as "glue." Serve on lettuce leaves, if you'd like. Makes 6 servings

FOR 1 SERVING: CALORIES 138 (45% from fat); FAT 6.9g (sat 1.4g, mono 0g, poly 0.1g); PROTEIN 1.1g; CARB 19g; FIBER 2.5g; CHOL 7mg; IRON 0.5mg; SODIUM 212mg; CALC 31mg

* see glossary

SIMON THE CENTIPEDE

"It was fun mixing up the green stuff. I'd love to make this again, and when I do, I might use a different color for the icing." —Taylor, Age 6

1 (8-ounce) **container frozen whipped topping**, thawed

½ to 1 teaspoon **green liquid food coloring**

36 **vanilla wafers**

1 **banana**, peeled and cut into 36 slices

Decorations: miniature candy-coated chocolate pieces (we used M&M's minis), 1 cherry-flavored chewy fruit roll (we used Fruit Rollups), 6 uncooked spaghetti strands, pull-and-peel red candy ropes (we used Twizzlers), crumbled cream-filled chocolate sandwich cookies (optional)

1 • Place whipped topping in a medium bowl; gently *fold** in food coloring.

2 • Place 1 teaspoon whipped topping on the flat side of 1 vanilla wafer; top with a banana slice. Do the same thing all over again with the whipped topping, vanilla wafers, and banana slices. You'll have 36 stacks.
 • Put 6 stacks together in a row to make a log. Curve log slightly, if you'd like. Do the same thing all over again with the remaining stacks. *Spread** remaining whipped topping on each log. Cover and *chill** in the refrigerator at least 8 hours.

3 • Attach chocolate pieces to logs to resemble eyes and spots.
 • Cut fruit roll into small pieces, and attach to logs to resemble mouths.

To make the antennae and legs:
 • Snap spaghetti strands in half. Separate candy ropes into strands. Cut strands into 12 (7-inch) segments. Tie a loose knot into 1 candy strand close to the end. Insert the tip of 1 strand of spaghetti into the knot, and carefully tighten. Starting at the knot, wind the candy strand around the spaghetti pressing gently as you go so the candy will stick to the spaghetti. Break the spaghetti off about an inch below the strand. Do the same thing all over again with the remaining 11 (7-inch) segments of candy and spaghetti. Insert into the logs just above the eyes to resemble antennae.
 • Separate more candy ropes into thin strands. Cut strands into 6 dozen (1-inch) segments, and stick them into sides of logs to resemble legs.

4 • Serve on a bed of crumbled cream-filled sandwich cookies, if you'd like. Makes 6 servings

FOR 1 SERVING: CALORIES 282 (41% from fat); FAT 13g (sat 6.6g, mono 0g, poly 0g); PROTEIN 2.6g; CARB 36.3g; FIBER 0.5g; CHOL 6mg; IRON 1.4mg; SODIUM 156mg; CALC 1mg

* see glossary

Note: This cute dessert tastes a lot like banana pudding. The crisp vanilla wafers soften as it chills overnight, so it's perfect to eat with a spoon.

PUDDIN' HEADS

Look how easy it is to go from a plain dessert to one that is utterly amusing! The sky's the limit when it comes to edible choices for funny facial features. Use those pictured below, or be creative and discover your own.

Simple Vanilla Pudding
(page 132)

Decorations: cereal, grapes, blueberries, orange slices, strawberries, kiwifruit, gumdrops

1 • Spoon Simple Vanilla Pudding into a serving bowl, and use decorations to create fun faces. Makes 4 servings

FOR 1 SERVING: CALORIES 143 (25% from fat); FAT 4g (sat 2.3g, mono 1g, poly 0.2g); PROTEIN 4g; CARB 22.7g; FIBER 0.2g; CHOL 12mg; IRON 0.1mg; SODIUM 122mg; CALC 140mg

Note: Breakfast foods like cream of wheat and oatmeal are also fun to eat when they're transformed into happy faces.

**Prep: 35 min.
Cook: 20 min.**

BEARY GOOD ROLLS

They're so cute, you'll want to eat 'em up!

Cinnamon Raisin Bread
dough (page 42)

1 **large egg,** well beaten

1 tablespoon **water**

Currants or raisins

1 (4.25-ounce) **tube white
decorating icing with
piping tip** (we used
Betty Crocker)

1 • Prepare Cinnamon Raisin Bread dough through step 2, omitting raisins.

2 • Preheat* oven to 350°.

3 • Whisk* together egg and water in a small bowl. Set aside.
• Divide* dough into 6 equal portions. Divide each portion into 8 balls
as follows: 1 (2½-inch) ball for body, 1 (1½-inch) ball for head,
4 (¾-inch) balls for arms and legs, and 2 (½-inch) balls for ears.
Assemble bears on a lightly greased* baking sheet using egg mixture
to "glue" bear together. Brush bears with egg mixture, and attach
currants as shown in photograph.

4 • Bake* at 350° for 18 to 20 minutes or until golden. Remove baking
sheet from the oven using oven mitts. Cool on a wire rack.
• Squeeze icing onto rolls as shown in photograph. Makes 6 rolls

FOR 1 ROLL: CALORIES 421 (20% from fat); FAT 9.5g (sat 0.6g, mono 3g, poly 1.9g); PROTEIN 8.3g;
CARB 75.4g; FIBER 2.5g; CHOL 18mg; IRON 3.2mg; SODIUM 447mg; CALC 24mg

* see glossary

HOMEMADE PLAY DOUGH

This play dough smells delicious, but it doesn't taste very good. Don't eat it—it's just for molding, shaping, and squishing.

1½ cups **all-purpose flour**

1 tablespoon **cream of tartar**

¾ teaspoon **salt**

1½ cups **water**

1½ tablespoons **vegetable oil**

1½ teaspoons **peppermint, lemon, vanilla, or almond extract**

Food coloring paste

1
- *Whisk** together first 6 ingredients in a big saucepan; place over medium heat. Cook 4 to 5 minutes, stirring constantly and vigorously, until mixture separates from the sides of the pan and forms a ball.
- Remove dough from saucepan; let it sit on the countertop until cool (about 5 minutes). *Knead** dough until smooth and silky. Knead in food coloring paste to desired color. (*Divide** the dough into portions, and tint each portion a different color, if you'd like.)

2
- Enjoy playing with the Homemade Play Dough.
- When you're done, store it in the refrigerator in an airtight container up to 1 week. Makes about 2 cups

* see glossary

Tip: A tiny bit of food coloring paste goes a long way. Dip a wooden pick into the paste, and rub it over the top of the dough before kneading it in. You can always add more, if you'd like.

DOGGIE TREATS

MAKE-AHEAD

JUST FOR FUN

"My dog stayed in the kitchen while we made these. As soon as the first batch was cool, she got to try one. She grabbed it like it was a steak bone." —Luke, Age 7

½ cup **quick-cooking oats**

2 tablespoons **butter or margarine**

¾ cup very hot **water**

1 (2.5-ounce) **jar beef baby food** (we used Gerber)

1 **large egg**

¼ cup **instant nonfat dry milk**

¼ cup (1 ounce) shredded **Cheddar cheese**

1½ cups **whole wheat flour**

½ cup **yellow cornmeal**

½ cup **wheat germ**

⅛ teaspoon **salt**

1 • *Preheat** oven to 350°.

2 • *Stir** together first 3 ingredients in a big bowl, and let stand 10 minutes. Add baby food and next 3 ingredients, stirring until blended. Add remaining ingredients; stir mixture until a stiff dough forms.
• *Roll** dough to ½-inch thickness on a lightly floured surface. Cut with a 2- to 4-inch cookie cutter. Place on lightly *greased** baking sheets.

3 • *Bake** at 350° for 12 to 16 minutes or until lightly browned and firm. Remove baking sheets from the oven using oven mitts. Cool treats completely on a wire rack. Makes 1½ dozen

Kitty Treats:
• Stir in 2 tablespoons dried catnip with flour mixture in step 2. Continue as directed.

* see glossary

Tip: This recipe is completely safe and wholesome but intended to be eaten by dogs and cats. To keep up to **2 months**, freeze in a zip-top freezer bag.

Giant Barbecue
Bacon Burger
(page 180)

PARTY TIME

a BUGGY BIRTHDAY BASH

These boys couldn't resist inviting dozens of creepy crawlers to their celebration. And their friends couldn't resist the outrageous burger and party food!

MENU FOR 6
- Giant Barbecue Bacon Burger
- Creamy Salsa and tortilla chips
- Watermelon wedges
- Fruit sodas
- Candy Bar Cake

Clockwise from top: Candy Bar Cake (page 181), Giant Barbecue Bacon Burger (page 180), Creamy Salsa and tortilla chips (page 180), watermelon wedges, and fruit sodas

Giant Barbecue Bacon Burger

(pictured on page 179)

Don't let your eyes deceive you. This oversize burger will feed up to 6 partygoers after it's cut into generous wedges.

Prep: 16 min. Cook: about 20 min.

2 tablespoons **butter or margarine**

½ cup finely chopped **onion**

1½ pounds **lean ground beef**

⅓ cup **quick-cooking oats**

1 **large egg**

¼ cup **barbecue sauce**

¾ teaspoon **salt**

⅛ teaspoon **pepper**

6 **bacon slices,** cooked

4 (1-ounce) **processed American cheese slices**

1 (9-inch) **round bread loaf,** unsliced

¼ cup **barbecue sauce**

4 **lettuce** leaves

1 **tomato,** sliced

¼ cup **dill pickle slices**

1 • Ask a grown-up to prepare the grill.

2 Prepare the burger patty:
• Place butter in a big microwave-safe bowl. Cover with wax paper, and microwave at HIGH 30 seconds or until butter melts. *Stir** in onion. Cover and microwave at HIGH 2 more minutes or until onion is *tender**. Cool.

• Add beef, oats, egg, ¼ cup barbecue sauce, salt, and pepper; *mix** well.
• Turn beef mixture out onto a big piece of aluminum foil, and shape into a 9-inch patty.

3 • Grill patty, covered with grill lid, over medium-high heat (350° to 400°) 8 minutes on each side or until no longer pink, using a wide spatula to turn. Arrange bacon and cheese on patty the last 2 minutes of cooking.

4 Assemble the burger:
• Cut loaf of bread in half horizontally. *Spread** ¼ cup barbecue sauce over cut side of bottom half of bread.
• Arrange lettuce over barbecue sauce. Top with burger, tomato slices, and pickles. Cut burger into wedges to serve. Makes 6 servings

FOR 1 SERVING: CALORIES 540 (38% from fat); FAT 22.7g (sat 11.4g, mono 8.2g, poly 1.3g); PROTEIN 36.5g; CARB 49.2g; FIBER 1.6g; CHOL 131mg; IRON 5mg; SODIUM 1,484mg; CALC 120mg

* see glossary

Creamy Salsa

Creamy Salsa

Though usually made from yellow corn, tortilla chips can also be made from blue or red corn. Using the variety of colors turns this simple dip into something a bit more festive.

Prep: 5 min. Other: 1 hr.

1 (8-ounce) **carton sour cream**

1 cup **salsa**

¼ cup chopped **fresh cilantro**

2 teaspoons **ground cumin**

1 • Combine all ingredients in a medium-size bowl. *Stir** with a rubber spatula until blended. Cover and *chill** in refrigerator at least 1 hour or overnight.
• Serve with tortilla chips. Makes 2 cups

FOR 1 TABLESPOON: CALORIES 18 (80% from fat); FAT 1.6g (sat 0.9g, mono 0.4g, poly 0.1g); PROTEIN 0.4g; CARB 0.9g; FIBER 0.2g; CHOL 3mg; IRON 0.1mg; SODIUM 53mg; CALC 12mg

* see glossary

Candy Bar Cake

"I liked cutting up different kinds of candy bars and decorating the cake better than frosting it. My mom did that." —Seth, Age 9

**Prep: 35 min. Cook: 25 min.
Other: 1 hr., 10 min.**

- 1 (18.25-ounce) **package Swiss chocolate cake mix**
- 1 (8-ounce) **package cream cheese,** softened
- 1 cup **powdered sugar**
- ½ cup **granulated sugar**
- 1 (12-ounce) **container frozen whipped topping,** thawed
- 2 (2.07-ounce) **chocolate-coated caramel-peanut nougat bars**
- 2 (1.55-ounce) **milk chocolate bars with crisped rice**
- 1 (1.5-ounce) **crisp wafers in milk chocolate bar**

1 Make the cake layers:
- *Preheat* oven to 325°.
- Prepare cake batter according to package directions. Pour into 3 *greased* and floured 8-inch round cakepans.
- *Bake* at 325° for 20 to 25 minutes or until a wooden pick inserted in center comes out clean. Remove cake layers from the oven using oven mitts. Cool in pans on wire racks 10 minutes.
- Remove cake layers from pans, and cool completely on wire racks.

2 Prepare the frosting:
- *Beat* cream cheese, powdered sugar, and granulated sugar in a big bowl at medium speed with an electric mixer until sugar *dissolves* and mixture is creamy. *Fold* in whipped topping.

3 Frost and decorate the cake:
- *Spread* frosting between layers and on top and sides of cake.
- Cut candy bars into fun shapes, and press into frosting on top and sides of cake. Cover and *chill* at least 30 minutes or up to 1 day in advance. Makes 16 servings

FOR 1 SERVING: CALORIES 449 (47% from fat); FAT 23.6g (sat 10.2g, mono 6.7g, poly 4.3g); PROTEIN 4.9g; CARB 53.6g; FIBER 1.1g; CHOL 57mg; IRON 0.5mg; SODIUM 81mg; CALC 37mg

* see glossary

Note: We decorated our cake using Snickers, Nestlé Crunch, and Kit Kat candy bars.

Candy Bar Cake

JUST FOR GIRLS VALENTINE LUNCHEON

Gather special friends for this yummy menu, and you've got yourself a match made in heaven.

MENU FOR 6
- Ham and Cheese Party Sandwiches
- Peanutty Snack Mix
- Fresh strawberries
- Cranberry Lemonade Punch
- Notable Valentine Cupcakes

Notable Valentine
Cupcakes (page 185)

Ham and Cheese Party Sandwiches

Cut these sandwiches in half or quarters to show off the colorful layers and make them easier to hold.

Prep: 20 min. Other: 8 hrs.

- 6 **sandwich buns**, split
- 3 tablespoons **Italian dressing**
- 6 ounces thinly sliced **ham**
- 6 ounces thinly sliced **salami**
- 6 thin **provolone cheese** slices
- 6 small **Bibb lettuce** leaves
- 1 **small tomato**, thinly sliced
- ½ cup **garlic-and-herb spreadable cheese** (we used Alouette)

1 • Brush cut sides of each bun with dressing using a pastry brush. Arrange ham, salami, cheese, lettuce, and tomato on bottom halves of buns.
• *Spread** cut side of top halves of buns with spreadable cheese. Place top halves of buns, cheese side down, on each sandwich, pressing gently.
• Wrap sandwiches individually in plastic wrap, and *chill** in refrigerator overnight.

2 • To serve, unwrap sandwiches, and cut into quarters or halves, if you'd like. Makes 6 sandwiches

FOR 1 SANDWICH: CALORIES 402 (58% from fat); FAT 25.8g (sat 12.1g, mono 2.3g, poly 2.4g); PROTEIN 19.8g; CARB 22.8g; FIBER 1.2g; CHOL 61mg; IRON 1.7mg; SODIUM 1,054mg; CALC 209mg

* see glossary

Peanutty Snack Mix

You'll have enough of this crunchy snack to serve at the party and send a bag of it home with everyone as a party favor.

Prep: 5 min. Cook: 30 min.

- 1 (16-ounce) **jar unsalted dry-roasted peanuts**
- 1 (10-ounce) **package pretzel pieces**
- 1 (7-ounce) **can potato sticks**
- 1 (6-ounce) **can French fried onion rings** (we used French's)
- 1 (6-ounce) **package bite-size bagel chips**
- ⅓ cup **butter or margarine**, melted
- 1 (1.25-ounce) **package taco seasoning**

1 • *Preheat** oven to 250°.

2 • Combine first 5 ingredients in a big roasting pan. *Drizzle** with butter, gently stirring to coat. Sprinkle taco seasoning over peanut mixture, and gently *stir** to blend.
• *Bake** at 250° for 30 minutes, stirring occasionally. Remove pan from the oven using oven mitts. Carefully pour mixture onto paper towels, and cool. Store in an airtight container up to 1 week. Makes 12 cups

FOR ¼ CUP: CALORIES 152 (57% from fat); FAT 9.7g (sat 2.6g, mono 3g, poly 2.4g); PROTEIN 3.4g; CARB 13.6g; FIBER 1.3g; CHOL 3mg; IRON 0.8mg; SODIUM 244mg; CALC 7mg

* see glossary

Peanutty Snack Mix

Ham and Cheese Party Sandwiches

Cranberry Lemonade
Punch

Cranberry Lemonade Punch

A pink punch is a must for this feminine affair. Ice cubes made with cranberry juice keep it icy-cold and delicious.

Prep: 10 min. Cook: 5 min. Other: 1 hr.

> 2 cups **water**
>
> ½ cup **sugar**
>
> 1 (6-ounce) **can frozen lemonade concentrate,** thawed
>
> 3 cups **cranberry juice**
>
> 3 cups **water**

1• Combine 2 cups water and sugar in a small saucepan. Place over medium heat, and *stir** until sugar *dissolves**. Cool.

2• Combine sugar mixture, lemonade concentrate, cranberry juice, and 3 cups water in a big pitcher. *Chill** at least 1 hour. Makes 8 cups

FOR 1 CUP: CALORIES 131 (1% from fat); FAT 0.2g (sat 0g, mono 0g, poly 0.1g); PROTEIN 0.4g; CARB 34.1g; FIBER 0.1g; CHOL 0mg; IRON 0.4mg; SODIUM 3mg; CALC 9mg

* see glossary

Notable Valentine
Cupcakes

Notable Valentine Cupcakes

Secret notes written on scrolls of pretty paper deliver a Valentine message just before a yummy treat. Wooden picks and round gummy candies keep the notes from getting frosting on them.

Prep: 38 min. Cook: 22 min.

> 1 (18.25-ounce) **package strawberry-flavored cake mix**
>
> **Scrapbooking paper**
>
> 2 (16-ounce) **containers ready-to-spread vanilla frosting**
>
> **Red food coloring**
>
> **Colored sugar**
>
> 24 **roll-shaped chewy candies** (we used Gummi Savers)
>
> 24 **wooden party picks**

1• Prepare cake mix according to package directions for cupcakes.

2• While cupcakes cool, cut 24 (4- x ½-inch) strips of scrapbooking paper. Write Valentine notes on the plain side of each strip of paper. Beginning with a short side, roll up each strip tightly to hide the note. Set notes aside for now.

3• Spoon frosting into a big bowl, and *stir** in food coloring, 1 drop at a time, until the color is just what you'd like.

4Decorate the cupcakes:
• *Spread** cupcakes evenly with frosting. Sprinkle with colored sugar. Place 1 round gummy candy on each cupcake.
• Using picks, attach notes to cupcakes through the round gummy candies. Makes 2 dozen cupcakes

FOR 1 CUPCAKE: CALORIES 269 (25% from fat); FAT 7.6g (sat 1.6g, mono 2.3g, poly 3.5g); PROTEIN 1.2g; CARB 48.8g; FIBER 0g; CHOL 0mg; IRON 0.6mg; SODIUM 210mg; CALC 41mg

* see glossary

aPRiL* FOOLS' SUPPER

Outprank your family with this deliciously wacky meal. They'll love the recipes even more when they're served in unpredictable ways.

MENU FOR 4
- Meatloaf in a Mug
- Whole Roasted Carrots
- Wacky Mashed Potatoes
- Lemonade
- S'mores Sundaes

Clockwise from right: Meatloaf in a Mug (page 188), Wacky Mashed Potatoes (page 189), Whole Roasted Carrots (page 188)

Meatloaf in a Mug

Most meatloaves bake in pans in ovens for hours. But these bake up quick using microwave powers!

Prep: 12 min. Cook: 11 min. Other: 2 min.

- 1 pound **extra-lean (92% lean) ground beef**
- ½ cup **quick-cooking oats**
- 1 **large egg**
- 1 (5½-ounce) **can vegetable juice** (we used V-8)
- ¼ cup finely chopped **green onions**
- ¼ cup finely chopped **carrot**
- ½ teaspoon **salt**
- ¼ teaspoon **pepper**
- ¼ cup **ketchup**

1 • *Stir** together first 8 ingredients in a big bowl. *Divide** mixture evenly into 4 portions. Shape each portion into a ball. Place each ball into an 8-ounce microwave-safe coffee mug.

2 • Line the bottom of the microwave with a big sheet of wax paper in case juices from the meatloaves bubble out.
- Place mugs in a circle on top of wax paper. Cover mugs with another big sheet of wax paper.
- Microwave at MEDIUM-HIGH (70% power) 11 minutes. Cut into meatloaves with a knife and fork. If any are still pink inside, microwave them 30 seconds more and recheck for doneness.
- Carefully remove each mug from the microwave using oven mitts.

3 • *Spread** 1 tablespoon ketchup over each meatloaf; cover with wax paper, and let stand 2 minutes. Makes 4 servings

FOR 1 SERVING: CALORIES 246 (41% from fat); FAT 11.1g (sat 4.6g, mono 4.6g, poly 0.8g); PROTEIN 25g; CARB 13.6g; FIBER 1.7g; CHOL 114mg; IRON 3.5mg; SODIUM 653mg; CALC 28mg

* see glossary

Whole Roasted Carrots

Follow recipe for Carrot Fries on page 115 but skip step 2. *Bake** as directed in step 3. You might have to bake these carrots 3 to 5 minutes longer to make them *tender** and brown.

* see glossary

Meatloaf in a Mug

Wacky Mashed
Potatoes

S'mores
Sundaes

Wacky Mashed Potatoes

This serving suggestion is fun any day of the year. Let the mashed potatoes cool long enough so they'll mound up in the cones just like ice cream.

Prep: 5 min. Cook: 8 min. Other: 5 min.

2⅔ cups **frozen mashed potatoes**

1⅓ cups **milk**

½ (8-ounce) **container soft cream cheese**

3 **green onions,** sliced

½ teaspoon **salt**

¼ teaspoon **pepper**

4 **flat-bottomed ice cream cones** (optional)

1 • Prepare potatoes with milk according to package directions, stirring with a wire whisk. *Stir** in cream cheese, green onions, salt, and pepper. Let stand 5 minutes or until cool enough to mound.

• To serve, spoon mashed potatoes into ice cream cones, if you'd like. Makes 4 servings

FOR 1 SERVING: CALORIES 247 (55% from fat); FAT 15.1g (sat 9.1g, mono 0.7g, poly 0.2g); PROTEIN 6.7g; CARB 23.5g; FIBER 2.3g; CHOL 39mg; IRON 0.2mg; SODIUM 599mg; CALC 119mg

* see glossary

S'mores Sundaes

No campfire needed for this clever dessert. You can enjoy these familiar flavors year-round indoors!

Prep: 5 min. Cook: 2 min.

½ (12-ounce) **jar hot fudge sauce**

1 (7-ounce) **jar marshmallow cream**

1 pint **vanilla ice cream**

3 **graham cracker sheets,** separated

1 • Warm hot fudge sauce according to directions on jar.

• *Spread** marshmallow cream in the bottom of 4 (6-ounce) dessert bowls. Top with ice cream and hot fudge sauce. Serve with graham crackers. Makes 4 servings

FOR 1 SERVING: CALORIES 482 (24% from fat); FAT 13.1g (sat 6.7g, mono 2.6g, poly 0.7g); PROTEIN 4.5g; CARB 87.7g; FIBER 1.4g; CHOL 29mg; IRON 0.9mg; SODIUM 260mg; CALC 130mg

* see glossary

Tablesetting Tip: In the spirit of April Fools' Day, serve this menu using unexpected containers and serving utensils. Small toy buckets or canning jars stand in for ordinary glasses. Why not use a small spade or big serving forks and spoons? Take a look at your toys and around your kitchen for ideas. Of course, check with a grown-up to make certain your choices are a reasonable size, safe, and clean.

BACK-TO-SCHOOL *PIZZA PARTY

Know what's smarter than smart? A party to reunite school friends, cook up Custom Kid Pizzas, and sip on Cherry Cola Floats.

MENU FOR 8
- Chopped Italian Salad with Pepperoni
- Custom Kid Pizzas
- Cherry Cola Floats

Custom Kid Pizzas
(page 192)

Chopped Italian Salad with Pepperoni

Chopped salads are easy to eat because the ingredients are already cut into bite-size pieces.

Prep: 15 min.

- 1 (10-ounce) **bag romaine lettuce**
- ½ (8-ounce) **package sliced pepperoni,** halved
- ½ (8-ounce) **block mozzarella cheese,** cut into ½-inch cubes
- ¾ cup **reduced-fat Italian dressing**
- 2 tablespoons grated **Parmesan cheese**
- 2 **small tomatoes,** diced (optional)
- 1 (4½-ounce) **can sliced ripe black olives,** drained (optional)

1 • Place lettuce in a big salad bowl, and tear into bite-size pieces using your fingers. Top with pepperoni and mozzarella cheese.
- *Whisk** together Italian dressing and Parmesan cheese in a small bowl. Just before serving, *drizzle** Italian dressing mixture over lettuce, and *toss** to coat. Top salad with tomatoes and olives, if you'd like. Makes 8 servings

FOR 1 SERVING: CALORIES 156 (70% from fat); FAT 12.2g (sat 4.3g, mono 2.8g, poly 0.4g); PROTEIN 7.3g; CARB 3.8g; FIBER 1g; CHOL 25mg; IRON 0.6mg; SODIUM 715mg; CALC 129mg

* see glossary

Chopped Italian Salad with Pepperoni

Custom Kid Pizzas

(pictured on page 190)
Make the Pizza Dough and Pizza Sauce the day before the party.

Prep: 1 hr. Cook: 20 min. Other: 8 hrs.

Pizza Dough

Pizza Sauce

- 3 cups (12 ounces) **shredded pizza cheese blend**

Toppings: pepperoni slices, chopped red or green bell pepper, pineapple tidbits, cubed ham, sliced fresh mushrooms, sliced ripe black olives (optional)

1 • Let pizza dough balls stand at room temperature 15 minutes.

2 • *Preheat** oven to 450°.

3 Assemble the pizzas:
- Shape each Pizza Dough ball into a 6- to 8-inch circle on parchment paper.
- *Spread** 2 tablespoons Pizza Sauce over each crust. Sprinkle each pizza with about ⅓ cup cheese. Add toppings, if you'd like. Slide pizzas onto baking sheets using parchment paper.

4 • *Bake** at 450° on lowest oven rack for 15 minutes or until browned. Remove baking sheets from the oven using oven mitts. Makes 8 pizzas

FOR 1 PIZZA: CALORIES 497 (31% from fat); FAT 17.1g (sat 6.9g, mono 3.1g, poly 3.3g); PROTEIN 19.8g; CARB 65.1g; FIBER 3.7g; CHOL 30mg; IRON 4.4mg; SODIUM 835mg; CALC 338mg

Pizza Dough

- 1½ cups warm **water** (100° to 110°)
- 2 (¼-ounce) **envelopes active dry yeast**
- 2 tablespoons **sugar**
- 4½ cups **all-purpose flour**
- 1 teaspoon **salt**
- ¼ cup **vegetable oil**
- **Vegetable cooking spray**

1• Place warm water in a small bowl. Sprinkle *yeast** and sugar over water, stirring until they *dissolve**. Let stand 5 minutes or until mixture is bubbly.

2• Combine flour and salt in a big bowl; make a *well** in center of mixture. Pour yeast mixture and oil into well, and *stir** to form a soft dough. Turn dough out onto a lightly floured surface, and *knead** 5 minutes.
• Spray inside of a big bowl with cooking spray, and place dough inside it. Lightly spray top of dough. Cover with plastic wrap, and refrigerate overnight.

3• Overnight the dough will *rise** and double in size. Punch dough down with your fist to release air. *Divide** dough into 8 equal portions, shaping each into a 3-inch ball. Loosely wrap each ball in plastic wrap, and chill in refrigerator. Makes 8 dough balls

FOR 1 DOUGH BALL: CALORIES 333 (21% from fat); FAT 7.8g (sat 0.9g, mono 3.1g, poly 3.3g); PROTEIN 7.9g; CARB 57.5g; FIBER 2.3g; CHOL 0mg; IRON 3.6mg; SODIUM 293mg; CALC 12mg

Pizza Sauce

- 1 (8-ounce) **can tomato sauce with garlic, oregano, and basil**
- 1 (6-ounce) **can tomato paste**
- ¼ teaspoon **pepper**

1• *Stir** together all ingredients in a saucepan. Bring to a *boil** over medium-high heat; reduce heat to low, and *simmer**, stirring occasionally, 5 minutes. Makes 1 cup

FOR 2 TABLESPOONS: CALORIES 29 (9% from fat); FAT 0.3g (sat 0g, mono 0g, poly 0.1g); PROTEIN 1.4g; CARB 6.1g; FIBER 1.4g; CHOL 0mg; IRON 0.8mg; SODIUM 257mg; CALC 26mg

* see glossary

Cherry Cola Floats

Before the excitement of the party begins, assemble these dessert-like beverages through step 1, and keep them in the freezer up to 1 hour in advance. Just before serving, fill them with cola.

Prep: 10 min.

- 1 (10-ounce) **jar maraschino cherries with stems,** undrained
- ½ gallon **vanilla ice cream**
- 4 (12-ounce) **cans cola soft drink**

1• *Drain** maraschino cherries, reserving juice. Set cherries aside for now.
• *Divide** maraschino cherry juice evenly among 8 glasses.

Top with 1 cup ice cream.

2• Slowly fill each glass with cola soft drink. Top floats with cherries. Makes 8 servings

FOR 1 SERVING: CALORIES 350 (37% from fat); FAT 14.5g (sat 9g, mono 4.2g, poly 0.5g); PROTEIN 4.6g; CARB 54.7g; FIBER 0g; CHOL 58mg; IRON 0.2mg; SODIUM 113mg; CALC 171mg

* see glossary

Cherry Cola Floats

FALL FESTIVAL BLOCK PARTY

Invite the kids to come in costume, if you'd like, and award blue ribbons to all. Categories like most creative, funniest, best of show, and scariest make everyone winners.

MENU FOR 8

• White Chicken Stew Brew
• Pumpkin Cheese Ball
• Monster Eyes
• Corny Candy Popcorn Balls
• Chocolate Spiderweb Treats
• Spiced Pear Cider

Pumpkin Cheese Ball (page 196)

Corny Candy Popcorn
Balls (page 198)

Chocolate Spiderweb Treats
(page 199)

White Chicken Stew Brew

Prepare up to 2 days in advance, and refrigerate. Reheat over low heat, stirring frequently. If it's too thick, stir in a little water.

Prep: 15 min. Cook: 33 min.

- 1 tablespoon **butter or margarine**
- 3 **carrots,** peeled and chopped
- 1 **large onion,** chopped
- 1 teaspoon **bottled minced garlic**
- 1 **rotisserie chicken,** skinned, boned, and coarsely chopped
- 2 (14-ounce) **cans chicken broth**
- 1 (4.5-ounce) **can chopped green chiles**
- 1 teaspoon **ground cumin**
- ⅛ teaspoon **ground red pepper**
- 3 (16-ounce) **cans great Northern beans,** rinsed and drained
- ½ cup **whipping cream**
- ¼ cup chopped **fresh cilantro** (optional)

1 • *Melt** butter in a Dutch oven over low heat; add carrot, onion, and garlic. *Sauté** until *tender**.
• Stir in chicken, chicken *broth**, green chiles, cumin, and red pepper; bring to a *boil** over medium-high heat. Reduce heat, cover, and *simmer** 20 minutes.

2 • Place beans in a medium bowl, and *mash** using a potato masher until about half the beans are still whole.

White Chicken Stew Brew

• Add beans and whipping cream to chicken mixture. Cook 10 minutes over medium heat, stirring frequently, until thickened and hot. Stir in cilantro, if you'd like. Makes 8 cups

FOR 1 CUP: CALORIES 258 (39% from fat); FAT 11.2g (sat 5g, mono 3.2g, poly 1g); PROTEIN 21.5g; CARB 20.6g; FIBER 6.1g; CHOL 75mg; IRON 2.2mg; SODIUM 1,014mg; CALC 70mg

* see glossary

Pumpkin Cheese Ball

(pictured on page 194)

There's no pumpkin in this cheese ball—it's just shaped like one!

Prep: 12 min. Other: 1 hr.

- 2 (8-ounce) **packages shredded extra-sharp Cheddar cheese**
- 1 (8-ounce) **package cream cheese,** softened
- 1 (8-ounce) **container chive-and-onion cream cheese**
- 2 teaspoons **paprika**
- ½ teaspoon **ground red pepper**

  Paprika (optional)
- 1 **broccoli stalk**

1 • Combine Cheddar cheese, cream cheeses, 2 teaspoons paprika, and red pepper in a big bowl. *Beat** at medium speed with an electric mixer until blended. Cover with plastic wrap, and *chill** at least 1 hour.

2 • Shape cheese mixture into a ball, and place on a flat serving plate. Make vertical grooves in ball using the handle of a wooden spoon to resemble a pumpkin, and dust grooves with paprika, if you'd like. Cover cheese ball with plastic wrap, and refrigerate up to 5 days.
• Cut florets from broccoli; save them to eat later. Trim small leaves from broccoli stalk. Cut stalk to look like a pumpkin stem; press into top of cheese ball along with small leaves from broccoli. Serve with apple wedges or crackers. Makes 4 cups

FOR 1 TABLESPOON: CALORIES 53 (78% from fat); FAT 4.6g (sat 3.1g, mono 0.4g, poly 0.1g); PROTEIN 2.1g; CARB 0.6g; FIBER 0g; CHOL 15mg; IRON 0.1mg; SODIUM 71mg; CALC 58mg

* see glossary

Monster Eyes

Beware—these goofy sausage
balls stare back!

Prep: 30 min. Cook: 22 min.

> 3 cups **all-purpose baking mix**
>
> 1 pound **ground mild or hot pork sausage**
>
> 1 (10-ounce) **block extra-sharp Cheddar cheese**, shredded (we used Cracker Barrel)
>
> 54 **small pimiento-stuffed olives**

1 • *Preheat** oven to 400°.

2 • Combine baking mix, sausage, and cheese in a big bowl. *Stir** with a wooden spoon until blended.

3 • Shape sausage mixture into 1-inch balls, and place on lightly *greased** baking sheets. Press 1 olive deeply into each ball. Reroll using the palms of your hands if you need to reshape.
• *Bake** at 400° for 22 minutes or until lightly browned. Remove baking sheets from the oven using oven mitts. Makes about 4½ dozen Monster Eyes

FOR 1 MONSTER EYE: CALORIES 54 (57% from fat); FAT 3.4g (sat 1.4g, mono 1g, poly 0.3g); PROTEIN 2.6g; CARB 3.7g; FIBER 0.3g; CHOL 9mg; IRON 0.3mg; SODIUM 176mg; CALC 55mg

* see glossary

Make-Ahead Tip: Freeze Monster Eyes in an airtight container up to 1 month. To reheat, place frozen balls on an ungreased baking sheet, and bake at 350° for 10 minutes or until heated through.

A pumpkin hunt is fun! Before everyone gathers, hide miniature pumpkins. Award a prize to the kid who finds the most.

Monster Eyes

Corny Candy Popcorn Balls

Full of popcorn, teddy bear cookies, and candy corn and glued together by melted marshmallows, this treat will be a hit. You'll need to work quickly to shape the balls, so gather everyone to help.

Prep: 25 min. Cook: 5 min.

50	large marshmallows
⅓	cup **butter or margarine**
20	cups freshly popped **popcorn**
2	cups **teddy bear-shaped chocolate graham cracker cookies**
2½	cups **candy corn**
	Vegetable cooking spray

1· Combine marshmallows and butter in a Dutch oven. Cook over medium-low heat until melted and smooth, stirring occasionally. Remove from heat.

2· Combine popcorn and graham cracker cookies in a big bowl. Pour marshmallow mixture over popcorn mixture, tossing to coat. *Stir** in candy corn.
· Spray hands with cooking spray, and shape popcorn mixture into 3-inch balls, pressing together firmly. Cool on wax paper. Wrap balls in plastic wrap. Store in an airtight container up to 3 days. **Makes 20 popcorn balls**

FOR 1 POPCORN BALL: CALORIES 241 (18% from fat); FAT 4.7g (sat 2.3g, mono 0.9g, poly 0.3g); PROTEIN 2g; CARB 49.3g; FIBER 1.5g; CHOL 8mg; IRON 0.6mg; SODIUM 89mg; CALC 31mg

Corny Candy
Popcorn Balls

Chocolate
Spiderweb Treats

Chocolate Spiderweb Treats

In step 4, it's best to start by snipping a very tiny hole in the corner of the plastic bag. If it's too small, you can always make it bigger.

**Prep: 35 min. Cook: 5 min.
Other: 35 min.**

> 4 cups firmly packed **miniature marshmallows**
>
> ⅓ cup **creamy peanut butter**
>
> 2 tablespoons **butter or margarine**
>
> 6 cups **chocolate sweetened rice cereal** (we used Cocoa Krispies)
>
> 1 (12-ounce) **package milk chocolate morsels**
>
> ½ cup **white chocolate morsels**

1 • Combine marshmallows, peanut butter, and butter in a big microwave-safe bowl. Microwave at HIGH 2 minutes.

• Remove from the microwave using oven mitts. *Stir** peanut butter mixture vigorously with a wooden spoon until smooth. Add cereal, and stir until well coated.

• Quickly spoon mixture into a lightly *greased** 15- x 10-inch jelly-roll pan, and press into an even layer. Cool 5 minutes or until firm.

2 • Cut cereal mixture into circles with a 3-inch round cookie cutter. Store excess cereal mixture in an airtight container for snacking on later.

3 • Place milk chocolate morsels in a small microwave-safe glass bowl or measuring cup. Microwave at MEDIUM (50% power) 2 minutes or until chocolate looks like it's just beginning to *melt**. Stir chocolate until smooth.

4 • Place white chocolate morsels in a zip-top freezer bag. Partially seal bag, and set upright in a small microwave-safe measuring cup. Microwave at MEDIUM (50% power) 1 minute.

• Gently squeeze bag until smooth. *Snip** a tiny hole in 1 corner of bag to create a small opening.

5 • *Spread** melted milk chocolate over top of 1 circle. While milk chocolate is still soft, *drizzle** white chocolate in 3 rings on top of milk chocolate. Starting at the center, pull a wooden pick through the rings to create a "web." Do the same thing all over again with the remaining circles and chocolate. Refrigerate 30 minutes or until chocolate is firm.

• Store in an airtight container up to 3 days. Makes 1½ dozen treats

FOR 1 TREAT: CALORIES 215 (41% from fat); FAT 9.7g (sat 5.9g, mono 2.7g, poly 0.7g); PROTEIN 2.6g; CARB 32.2g; FIBER 1.3g; CHOL 2mg; IRON 0.6mg; SODIUM 85mg; CALC 2mg

* see glossary

Spiced Pear Cider

Spiced Pear Cider

If the weather is predicted to be warmer than usual, prepare this a day in advance, and chill. Serve it over crushed ice.

Prep: 5 min. Cook: 3 hrs.

> 16 whole **allspice**
>
> 8 whole **cloves**
>
> 4 (3-inch) **cinnamon sticks**
>
> 6 cups **unsweetened pear juice**
>
> 2 cups **pear nectar**

1 • Place allspice, cloves, and cinnamon in the center of a coffee filter or an 8-inch square of cheesecloth. Gather edges into a sack, and tie sack with a small piece of kitchen string.

• Combine spice sack, pear juice, and pear nectar in a 3-quart slow cooker. Cover with lid, and cook on LOW 3 hours.

2 • Throw away the spice bag. Serve hot. Makes 8 cups

FOR 1 CUP: CALORIES 125 (0% from fat); FAT 0g (sat 0g, mono 0g, poly 0g); PROTEIN 0.1g; CARB 32.1g; FIBER 0.6g; CHOL 0mg; IRON 0.2mg; SODIUM 3mg; CALC 26mg

HOLIDAY GOODIE SWAP

Invite your friends over to share a bounty of their own homemade treats. They'll have loads of fun nibbling on the assortment at the party and will love taking home a box brimming with pretty packages.

MENU
- Peanut Butter Stuffed Apples
- Santa Fe Snack Seeds
- Snowballs
- Peppermint Cookie Canes
- Hot chocolate

Peppermint Cookie
Canes (page 203)

Peanut Butter Stuffed Apples

(pictured on page 200)

For the sweetest apples, use Golden or Red Delicious. Wrap each apple in holiday cellophane, and tie with ribbon.

Prep: 30 min.

> 1 (8-ounce) **package cream cheese**, softened
> 1½ cups **peanut butter**
> ½ cup **powdered sugar**
> 12 **small apples**, unpeeled
> 1 cup **candy sprinkles, chopped peanuts, or graham cracker crumbs**

1 • Combine first 3 ingredients in a small mixing bowl; *beat** at medium speed with an electric mixer until smooth.
• Remove cores from apples using an apple corer.

2 • Using a small spoon, pack peanut butter mixture into core of each apple. *Dredge** open ends in candy sprinkles, chopped peanuts, or graham cracker crumbs.
• Wrap apples in plastic wrap, and store in refrigerator up to 2 days. Makes 12 stuffed apples

FOR 1 STUFFED APPLE: CALORIES 407 (50% from fat); FAT 22.8g (sat 7.2g, mono 1.9g, poly 0.3g); PROTEIN 9.7g; CARB 46.3g; FIBER 4.5g; CHOL 21mg; IRON 1.1mg; SODIUM 207mg; CALC 22mg

* see glossary

Note: Serve any remaining peanut butter mixture as a spread for apple slices or graham crackers.

Santa Fe Snack Seeds

Divide this hip food gift evenly among small airtight storage jars available from import or home stores.

Prep: 9 min. Cook: 9 min.

> ¼ cup **olive oil**
> 1 teaspoon **ground cumin**
> 1 teaspoon **chili powder**
> ¼ cup **sugar**
> 2 tablespoons **honey**
> 2 cups **pumpkin seeds**
> 2 cups **sunflower seeds**

1 • Heat oil in a large nonstick skillet until hot; add cumin and chili powder. Cook over medium-high heat 30 seconds, stirring constantly. Add sugar and honey, and stir until sugar *dissolves**.

2 • Stir in pumpkin and sunflower seeds; cook, stirring constantly, 8 minutes or until seeds are toasted and mixture smells good.

3 • Carefully spoon seed mixture onto a big piece of lightly *greased** aluminum foil. Cool completely.
• Store seeds in an airtight container up to 2 weeks. Makes 4 cups

FOR 2 TABLESPOONS: CALORIES 140 (74% from fat); FAT 11.5g (sat 1.5g, mono 2.1g, poly 3.1g); PROTEIN 4.7g; CARB 5.7g; FIBER 1.3g; CHOL 0mg; IRON 1.6mg; SODIUM 5mg; CALC 11mg

* see glossary

Tip: Use a funnel to fill the jars with the seed mix.

Santa Fe Snack Seeds

Snowballs

Snowballs

Beginning cooks can make these with little supervision. No knives or ovens are needed as long as the nuts are already chopped.

Prep: 25 min.

- 2¼ cups **chocolate sandwich cookie crumbs** (we used crumbs made from Oreo cookies)
- 1 cup **finely chopped pecans**
- ¾ cup sifted **powdered sugar**
- ⅓ cup **sweetened flaked coconut** (optional)
- ¼ cup **light corn syrup**
- ¼ cup **strawberry preserves**
- ¾ cup sifted **powdered sugar**

1 • Combine cookie crumbs, pecans, ¾ cup powdered sugar, and coconut, if you'd like, in a large bowl; add corn syrup and preserves. *Stir** until well blended.

2 • Shape mixture into 1-inch balls, using 1 level tablespoon of mixture for each. Roll balls in ¾ cup powdered sugar. Roll each ball again so it'll be coated very well. Store cookies in an airtight container up to 1 week. Makes about 28 cookies

FOR 1 COOKIE: CALORIES 111 (38% from fat); FAT 4.7g (sat 0.6g, mono 2.2g, poly 1.1g); PROTEIN 1g; CARB 17.4g; FIBER 0.7g; CHOL 0mg; IRON 0.7mg; SODIUM 85mg; CALC 3mg

* see glossary

Peppermint Cookie Canes

(pictured on page 200)
While shaping the cookies, keep the rest of the dough covered with plastic wrap so it won't dry out.

Prep: 25 min. Cook: 8 min. per batch Other: 15 min.

- ½ cup **butter**, softened
- ½ cup **shortening**
- 1½ cups **sugar**
- 1 **large egg**
- 1½ teaspoons **peppermint extract**
- ½ teaspoon **vanilla extract**
- 3½ cups sifted **cake flour**
- 1½ teaspoons **baking powder**
- ¼ teaspoon **salt**
- ¾ teaspoon **red food coloring paste**

1 • Combine butter and shortening in a big mixing bowl. *Beat** at medium speed with an electric mixer until creamy; gradually add sugar, beating well. Add egg, beating well. *Stir** in peppermint and vanilla extracts.
• Combine flour, baking powder, and salt; add to butter mixture, beating well.
• Remove half of dough from bowl. Add food coloring paste to dough in bowl, and *mix** until color is evenly distributed.

2 • Shape plain dough by teaspoonfuls into 4-inch ropes. Do the same thing with red dough.
• Place 1 red rope and 1 plain rope side by side; gently twist together. *Roll** twisted ropes into 1 rope. Shape into a cane, and place on an ungreased baking sheet. Do the same thing all over again with remaining ropes. *Chill** 15 minutes.

3 • *Preheat** oven to 375°.

4 • *Bake** at 375° for 8 minutes or just until lightly brown. Remove baking sheets from oven using oven mitts. Cool slightly. Carefully remove cookies to wire racks, using a spatula. Cool completely. Store cookies in an airtight container up to 1 week. Makes about 4 dozen cookies

FOR 1 COOKIE: CALORIES 87 (43% from fat); FAT 4.2g (sat 1.7g, mono 1.5g, poly 0.8g); PROTEIN 0.7g; CARB 11.8g; FIBER 0.1g; CHOL 9mg; IRON 0.6mg; SODIUM 42mg; CALC 11mg

* see glossary

GLOSSARY

Many words are identified in our recipes in *italics* with an asterisk (*) so you can look them up here if you don't know what they mean.

Bake To cook with dry heat in an oven.

Batter An uncooked mixture typically made from flour, eggs, and milk that can be spooned or poured.

Beat To mix ingredients by stirring quickly in a circular motion with a spoon, a fork, or an electric mixer.

Blend To mix ingredients together using a spoon, a blender, or an electric mixer.

Boil To cook at a temperature where bubbles break on the surface (212°F for water).

Broil To cook food directly under the heat source in an oven.

Broth A liquid made by simmering chicken, meat, seafood, or vegetables in water for a long time.

Chill To place food in the refrigerator to become firm or cold.

Chop To cut food into irregular small pieces.

Crisp-tender Used to describe cooked vegetables that are just tender but still have some snap.

Dissolve To mix a fine-textured substance, like sugar, into a liquid until the solid disappears.

Divide To split a portion of dough or ingredients into smaller portions, usually equal portions.

Drain To pour off liquid or fat using a colander or strainer, leaving solids behind.

Dredge To coat foods with an ingredient like flour, breadcrumbs, or chopped pecans.

Drizzle To pour a thin mixture over food in a thin stream.

Flip To turn something over, sometimes with a spatula and a quick twist of the wrist.

Fold To combine a light, airy mixture, like whipped topping, with a heavier mixture, like pudding, so that it stays puffy.

Grate To rub a piece of food, like cheese, across the surface of a grater covered with very small, sharp-edged holes.

Grease To rub the surface of a pan with fat, like butter or shortening, to prevent food from sticking, or to spray the surface with vegetable cooking spray.

Invert To turn a piece of cookware or a dish upside down so that the food falls out.

Juicer A kitchen tool or appliance used to remove juice from fruit.

Knead Pressing, folding, and turning dough with your hands to make it smooth and stretchy.

Marinate Soaking a food, like meat or vegetables, in a liquid mixture in the refrigerator so that the food will absorb the flavors and/or become tender.

Mash To squash or press down on a food, like bananas or cooked potatoes, with a fork or potato masher into an even consistency.

Melt To heat a solid food, like chocolate or butter, until it becomes liquid.

Mix To stir together dry or liquid ingredients until blended.

Pinch The small amount of a dry ingredient, like salt or pepper, that you can pick up, or "pinch," between your fingers.

Preheat To heat an oven, grill, or griddle to the correct temperature before using it.

Rind The thin, brightly colored outer layer of citrus fruits like lemons, limes, and oranges. Rind is most often grated.

Rise What happens to a dough or batter when it swells and puffs out because gas is released by the leavening ingredient like yeast, baking powder, or baking soda.

Roll To flatten dough with a rolling pin until it's even and smooth or to shape portions of dough into a rope.

Room temperature The temperature of a room that's not too hot or not too cold.

Sauté To quickly cook and stir food, like onion or garlic, in a small amount of oil or melted butter until it's tender and smells good.

Serving The amount of food served to one person.

Set When a fluid mixture, dough, or batter becomes more solid as it cooks or cools.

Shred To rub a piece of food, like cheese, across the surface of a grater covered with medium to large, sharp-edged holes.

Simmer To cook gently at a temperature just below boiling point.

Snip To cut into a tiny piece or pieces with kitchen shears.

Soften To let an ingredient, like butter, cream cheese, or ice cream, sit at room temperature long enough to become soft.

Spread To coat a food, like cake or cookies, with an even layer of a soft mixture, like frosting or jam.

Stir To blend ingredients by stirring in a circular motion with a spoon or fork.

Stir-fry To quickly cook small pieces of food, like meat and vegetables, in a big pan over high heat while stirring constantly.

Tender Used to describe food that's cooked until soft enough to cut and chew easily but not mushy.

Thaw To make frozen food melt.

Toss To mix something, like a salad, by lifting and turning the ingredients rather than stirring.

Well A hole that's made in a mixture of dry ingredients just before the liquid ingredients are added.

Whisk A tool made of looped wires that are attached to a handle. To whisk something means to make a soft or liquid mixture smooth or thick by beating it with a whisk or fork.

Yeast Microscopic plants that make bread rise.

RECIPE INDEX

SUBJECT INDEX